THE
PALESTINE
DECEPTION.

" England is far and honour a name."
NEWBOLT.

By
J. M. N. JEFFRIES.

LONDON:
CARMELITE HOUSE, E.C.4.

ISBN: 978-2-925611-48-6
Printed in the USA.

www.ultimatumeditions.com

THE
PALESTINE DECEPTION

"Daily Mail" Inquiry on the Spot

BY

J. M. N. JEFFRIES.

CONTENTS.

PAGE

ZIONIST CLAIMS REFUTED—PHANTOM BENEFITS FOR THE EMPIRE .. 11

"NATIONAL HOME" FOR THE JEWS—INSINCERITY AND ILLUSION .. 15

BRITISH JEWS OVERRULED—FORCING POLITICAL ZIONISM ON PALESTINE 22

THE BALFOUR DECLARATION—PROMISES WHICH MEAN NOTHING .. 27

CONTRADICTORY PLEDGES—MISLEADING THE ARABS 33

BROKEN FAITH WITH THE ARABS—McMAHON LETTERS DISCLOSURES .. 38

MR. CHURCHILL INVENTS A PROVINCE—PLEDGE IN WASTE-PAPER
BASKET 43

WHEEDLING THE PEACE CONFERENCE—EXTREME CLAIMS BY THE
ZIONISTS 47

ZIONIST DICTATORS—AN INTOLERABLE SITUATION 52

THE MANDATE PUZZLE—CIVIL GOVERNMENT INSTALLED.. 56

THE SLAV JEWS IN POWER—THE COMMUNIST ELEMENT 62

ENTER M. RUTENBERG—THE BLEAK FACTS TO-DAY 68

PAGE

MAP OF SYRIA 10

INTRODUCTION.

IN this series of articles Mr. J. M. N. Jeffries, the special correspondent of *The Daily Mail* has reported the results of his prolonged and systematic inquiries in Palestine into the financial position there and the attitude of the people to the Zionist régime.

Mr. Jeffries was admirably equipped for such an investigation. During the war he served as War Correspondent in the Near East, and after the war he paid various visits to Palestine, so that he knows that country as it was before the Zionist régime, and its problems. An experienced and careful inquirer, he spent many weeks in the mandated area last year ascertaining the facts. These he has now given to the public; and they throw a flood of new light on the Palestine situation and lead to certain inevitable conclusions, following as they do on the similar reports made for *The Daily Mail* by Sir Percival Phillips last year on the position in Mesopotamia.

The first conclusion is that *British Policy in this business of the Near East and Middle East mandates is entirely wrong.* Mr. Bonar Law admitted on November 7 last year that he wished "we had never gone to Mesopotamia," and he said some days earlier that he was being "bombarded" with requests from the British public to "go out of Mesopotamia and Palestine." In fact, the evacuation of these regions would be hailed with intense relief by the whole country as an escape from constant risk of complications and war and from an expenditure which the nation can no longer afford.

Behind all our difficulties with Turkey are the questions of Mosul, Mesopotamia, and Palestine. We might have claimed these countries on the ground of conquest, but we did not. We claim them because the League of Nations has handed them over to us. But the League has no right to do this. Its action was entirely illegal, as it had not consulted the Turks. Moreover, the alleged mandate which it issued to us to establish a National Home for Jews in Palestine struck at the first principle which the League professes to uphold—namely, self-determination.

Mr. Jeffries has shown, however, that *the mandate does not really exist*, and that *our presence in Palestine is based on an elaborate system of deception* and political fraud, for which the unfortunate British public have to pay the bills.

Two arguments have been advanced for our continued presence in Palestine, and both have been effectively answered by Mr. Jeffries. The first is that we must remain there because of our pledges. As a matter of fact, Mr. Jeffries has proved that a whole series of contradictory promises has been given to the population of Palestine. The first pledge was that of 1915, when the Arabs were guaranteed independence and the possession of Palestine. The Balfour Declaration was not made till November 2, 1917, and was in flagrant contradiction with this older promise, as it asserted the British Government's sympathy with the Jewish " National Home." The third pledge was that of November 1918, for " the establishment of national Governments and Administrations, deriving their authority from the initiative and free choice of the indigenous population," and was again contradictory of the Balfour Declaration.

So far as our pledges go, we ought to evacuate Palestine at once and not remain there. We ought, that is to say, to fulfil our first and earliest promise to the Arabs, who are seven-eighths of the population of Palestine, and give them independence, instead of trying to force on them with our aircraft and bayonets the rule of a mere fraction of Zionists.

The second argument is that we owe it as a duty to humanity to remain, and that in any case we are bound by the mandate (which, as has already been seen, does not exist). The best answer to this argument is to point out that the *United States was importuned to accept the mandate for Armenia. It refused to do so* as the American people would not take the risk of constant complications and heavy expenditure in Asia.

But there is a broader and stronger reason for evacuation. The British Empire has waxed great by "governing men as they wish to be governed." It is not doing this to-day in Palestine or Mesopotamia. In Palestine it is trying to foist on the Arabs the Zionist régime. In Mesopotamia and Kurdistan it is forcing on the population the alien régime of King Feisal. If we persist in this policy, then it may be predicted with certainty that nothing but embarrassment, war, and ruinous expenditure await us in Western Asia.

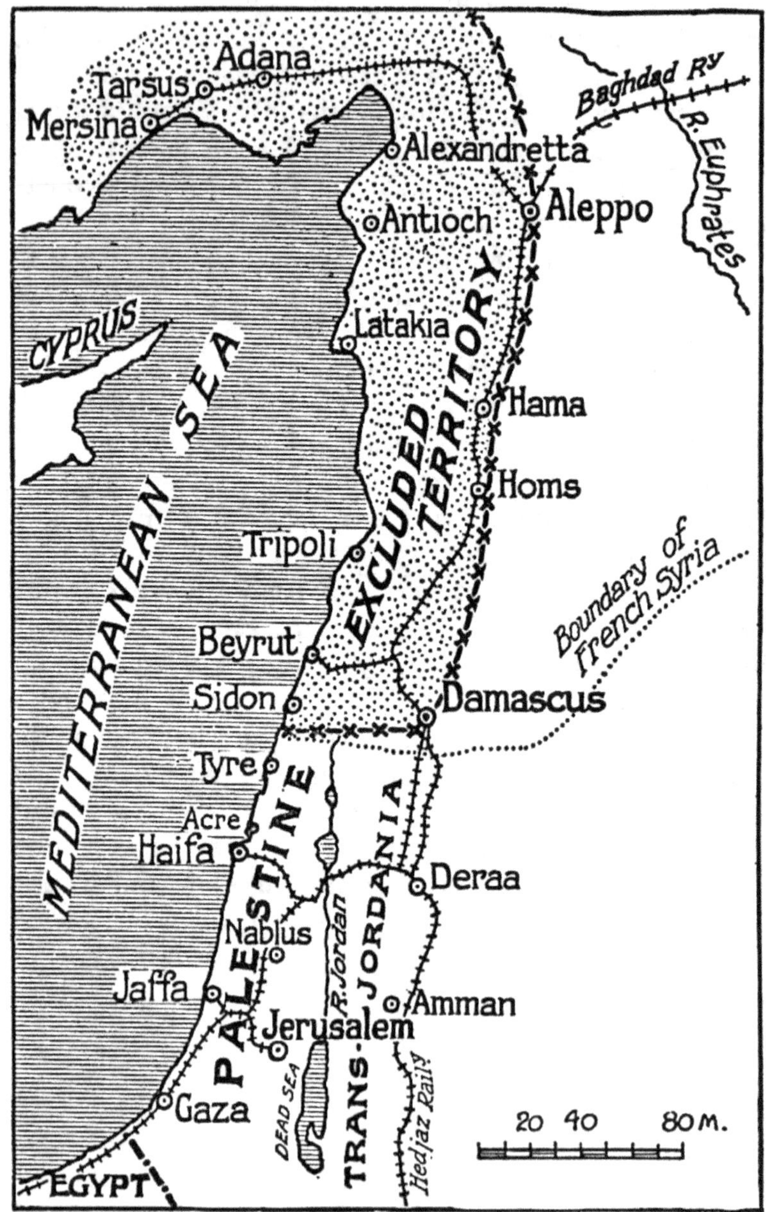

This Map shows the territory (unshaded) in Syria which was promised to the Arabs
by Sir H. McMahon in 1915. It will be seen that the unshaded portion includes all
Palestine, as far as the Egyptian frontier, so that Palestine already belonged to the
Arabs, when in 1917 Lord Balfour agreed to make it a National Home for the Jews.

ZIONIST CLAIMS REFUTED.

PHANTOM BENEFITS FOR THE EMPIRE.

There is no better way of summing up the whole Palestine position, as I now propose to do, than by taking, one by one, the various statements made by defenders of political Zionism and showing the amount of truth in them.

1. " England spends little or nothing in Palestine.'' England will have spent this year between Crown Agents' advances and upkeep of British gendarmerie at least £1,400,000.

2. " The Crown Agents' advances are against a loan which will be repaid by Palestine.'' This loan cannot be floated till the Mandate is ratified. One of the chief Allied Powers, whose consent would be necessary, will not ratify the Mandate in its present state. The people of Palestine will, if needs be, adopt universal passive resistance and refuse to pay taxes to redeem the advances till Zionist privilege has been removed. Till this occurs the loan will remain on British shoulders.

3. " Our soldiers will be removed from Palestine.'' Yes, plans are in existence at Jerusalem to remove the armoured cars, Air Force, and Indians, but even if this is done, there is the question of the British gendarmerie.

4. " The Palestine Government is effecting serious economies,'' The Government is one which contains some excellent officials, such as those now engaged upon an Economy Commitee, and they will propose the amalgamation of several departments, but there will still be a Budget of £2,000,000 for a population of 750,000. And the fact that there are four or five children in each Arab family must be remembered in estimating the onus of this.

5. " No Jewish immigrant has ever been a burden upon the people of the country.'' The presence of the Zionists, the standards they demand, the finding of labour upon public works for their immigrants, are a main cause of the existence of a

Government containing 41 effective departments, 362 senior officials, and the above mentioned Budget and debts, in a country the size of Wales.

6. " The presence of the Zionists has led to a spurt in British trade." Mr. Cowen and other apologists stress this point. On paper the value of British imports has increased considerably, but the enormously reduced value of money must be set against that. The imports total for the first nine months of 1922 about £1,100,000. The increase in British trade from pre-war days is about 10 per cent. The suggestion that Zionism is favouring British trade in particular is the usual propaganda. As between 1912 and 1922 Dutch imports increased from £7,000 to £44,000, Italian from £5,000 to £167,000, and German from £82,000 to £516,000, these increases being obtained on nine months of 1922 alone. As between the first and third quarters of 1922, British imports dropped nearly £100,000; German increased £20,000.

7. " A Zionist Palestine would be a limb or defence of the British Empire." Preposterous nonsense. In the nine months up to June last there were 63 British immigrants out of 7,015: 6,220 were from Poland, Ukraine, Russia, etc. The majority are only interested in Hebraism. Active non-British elements are amid them. One Kalvarisky, an important Zionist personage in Palestine, said on the occasion of a Ramazan reception, to the chief Syrian notable of Haifa :

" Why do you work against us? Give me your hand and let us work together against Europe, which wants to swallow us up together."

Two emissaries, one giving the name of Diamant, last December approached various Syrian notables to the same end. The phrase used to one was : " If you Arabs would only work with us Jews there would soon be no more of this Government, and of all these British ' types.' " These emissaries appeared as land surveyors.

8. " The National Home." Say rather the National Home from Home. The Zionist population is only maintained by constant immigration. Last spring and summer for every five Jews brought in one paid to go away. When the Government tried to get them to take up " Palestinian " nationality and surrender their national passports, they would not do it. To save

its face and form a voting register, the Government altered the formula, allowing them to retain their passports and actual nationality and be dimly enrolled as " Candidates for Prospective Palestinianism " at the same time. Can you beat it? as the Americans say.

9. " Palestine is the land of Israel." Whatever it was 2,000 years ago it is not so in that sense to-day. It is revolting that a Christian country such as Britain is should turn the Holy Land into a domain for free-thinking young Judæo-Slavs. Our forefathers made the Crusades; but our statesmen, fresh from sermons in the chapels of Wales, hand over the country of the Redeemer to infidels such as Richard Cœur de Lion never knew. I have no hesitation in saying that the " Halutzom," the young Zionist immigrants and intending masters of the country, have not a shred of belief. My own experience at the Colony of Nuris (370 colonists), for which Jews of the United States are being asked to subscribe, was eloquent.

" How do you manage without a synagogue? " I asked. " We don't have a synagogue; there's no religion here." The children are not brought up by their parents. I asked were not the little ones brought to their parents' tents at sundown, when the parents came in from work. " No."

" I suppose it's the lack of accommodation? " I suggested. " No," said my guide, " it's not in our ideas." Similar experiences recounted me by others visiting elsewhere. The old Jewish colony of Petah-Tikva an exception.

10. " No intention to oust the Arabs from Palestine." Zionist buyers have acquired about 290,000 acres, or one-seventh of the cultivable land of Palestine, already; a great deal on the instalment principle, and they may well now be unable to keep up their payments.

11. " Arabs are benefited by Zionist money spent in Palestine." See Statement 5. Arabs near Zionist colonies make some money from them, but the country at large, like the Zionists, is heading for bankruptcy. The imports of Palestine since the start of 1919 till the end of last September were £17,720,604; its exports but £3,044,225 ! What a picture ! In 1912 the surplus value of imports was £315,000, nothing of a total in comparison. Never very self-supporting, since Zionism and living beyond means

began on the grand scale, Palestine has practically lost all financial self-reliance, is fundamentally pauperised.

12. " Zionism's only desire is to benefit the country side by side with the Arabs." Just how many schemes for reconstructing the ports of Jaffa and Haifa have been held up in Jerusalem that " experts " might come out and examine, etc., though the greatest engineering firms in Britain offered to start straight away? More Rutenbergiana. Zionists or nobody.

13. " Zionism is taking the Jew from the ghetto and putting him on the land as a healthy farmer." Yes, and when a few decent, healthy farmers are created, as at Petah-Tikva, Zionism's banks are charging them 9 per cent. to a virtual 12 per cent. on loans to keep them going.

14. " The British Government must establish the National Home because that duty is laid upon it by the Palestine Mandate from the League of Nations." Hypocritical humbug. Who put it into the Mandate? And the *Mandate is not in force.*

15. " We must keep our word to the Zionists," given in the Balfour Declaration and the Churchill White Book. *We must not.* The Balfour Declaration and the White Book are both—I speak the truth—dishonest and fraudulent. We pledged ourselves through Sir Henry McMahon to an independent Arab kingdom, with boundaries including Palestine. No later promises in contradiction to that are of any value whatever; they are the second vows of bigamists. People who keep such vows have been dealt with by Tennyson :

> " His honour rooted in dishonour stood,
>   And faith unfaithful made them falsely true."

To Tennyson's countrymen I leave it to decide whether this shall be said of his country.

" NATIONAL HOME " FOR THE JEWS.

INSINCERITY AND ILLUSION.

Palestine to-day presents perhaps one of the finest opportunities which have ever been given to a British Government for repentance, even if that repentance be only for the deeds of its immediate predecessors in office. Those predecessors erred so greatly.

When in the course of the war, the members of our late Cabinet had to decide what should be the fate of the Holy Land and especially what part Great Britain was to play there, surely only one course was open to them. That was to be just and straightforward; to determine that on that sacred soil at least each word they uttered should bear nothing but its plain meaning, and each act be done for no other reason than the reason which openly they gave.

What they did was the exact opposite. They forced political Zionism on Palestine's unwilling people while pretending to leave their rights unimpaired. They let it be understood they were moved with deep sympathy with Zionism, whereas the sympathy with Zionism of most of them was mediocre, and in the case of one or two more akin to curiosity upon the results of a quaint experiment. Their real motives were not so much motives as the conclusion or carrying out of a bargain. They were guaranteed by Zionist leaders the support in the United States of those so-called German-Americans who had held aloof from the Allied Cause in return for the installing of Zionism in Palestine. This was a bargain which could not be honourably made since it involved the breaking of previous binding pledges to the Arab people, but they made it, none the less. At the same time they believed or deceived themselves into believing that by installing the Zionists in Palestine they would be establishing in a strategic corner of the Near East an extension or bulwark of the British Empire, would be installing as the guardians of Egypt and of British communications with India a body of our devoted friends.   They thought to place, as a mirthless Zionist propagandist once put it, " a little loyal Jewish Ulster amidst the enveloping hosts of Arabism."

While as an essay in plain speaking, our then Government produced as its gospel in Palestine the Balfour Declaration, a triumph of drafting of the plausible sort, in which deception is achieved by definition. A document which is not, as the general public believes, Lord Balfour's solitary emotional act, but the work of many minds, frequently modified and rearranged, as its British part-authors shrank from the frankness of the various texts which its Zionist part-authors provided.

What makes this poor artfulness of the late Cabinet the sadder, is that no one can say it was altogether successful in its own aims.   Zionist leaders claim that they were at the back of the withdrawal of German-American Jewish hostility to the Allies, and that it was through this and through them that our loans were obtained in the United States.   This is as it may be : I fancy many unhyphenated Americans would have a good deal to say about this.   While the world-financiers of Jewry, whose sympathy was sought by the Zionist move, do not appear to take much interest in Zionism, Baron Edmond de Rothschild, the one prominent Jew who has contributed generously out of great wealth, has always taken no part in political string-pulling.   And as for establishing a " strategic corner " for our benefit, the corner if left to itself would have been the first place to cleave to Britain.   We made the Arabs during the war, and until we imposed Zionism upon them, the Arabs of Palestine had throbbed for British occupation.   Even now they desire really British aid in governing that country, and at no cost to Britain.

What are we going to do there for them and for ourselves? Perhaps that will be best seen if I first give at due length the not very creditable story of what we have already done.   To understand to-day's conditions in Palestine you must first understand how they came about.

Our mistakes began early.   But the earliest of them, strangely enough, is one for which there is most degree of excuse, since in making it we were tied by arrangements with our Allies. This was the agreement negotiated in 1916 between Sir Mark Sykes on behalf of Great Britain and M. Picot on behalf of

France, under which British and French spheres of influence in the Near and Middle East were so divided that Syria was separated into three sections—British, French, and native, the northernmost French zone keeping the name of " Syria." The line of demarcation was termed the Sykes-Picot line, and it was assumed that certain of the southern sections of Syria would be internationalised.

Why this proposed internationalisation? Because those southern sections contained the Holy Places of Christendom. Palestine is nothing but the southern part of Syria. Our grandfathers, better read and informed in many ways than we are, were familiar with the name " Syria " as a country, and in their days many engravings and books of travel dealt with that country. The name had, of course, been handed down to them. Palestine had been recognised for generations as part of Syria, just as Sussex is part of England. The exigencies of the present half-mandatory system in the Near East have now, as it were, prised Palestine out of Syria and, for the sake of politico-Zionism in great part, driven us into creating the half-nationality of the Palestinian. But whatever names their not-quite-mandatories give to them, from Syria's northern point at Alexandretta to Gaza in the south, all the inhabitants of the land speak the same tongue, bear the same names, have the same appearance.

A man will live in Haifa in the British zone, his brother will be 80 miles away in Beyrut in the French zone, other brothers or cousins scattered up and down the country in Damascus or Jaffa or Aleppo. All these relatives under the Turkish régime, whether they were ill or well treated, were indistinguishably Syrians. They were great traders and travellers, and, as Syrians, travelled and traded and returned home.

But now these families are fitted with passports, for which they have to pay, and the traders are divided by Customs regulations, even if these have been made less vexatious lately, and are at the sport of rival tariffs. Brother George in Haifa is called a Palestinian, and brother Michael in Beyrut a real Syrian; they are of different mandatory nationality. The one might just as well have been called a Sykist and the other a Picotian, for any resemblance the division bears to reality.

If there were to be mandates in Syria elementary justice should have allowed the Syrians to give some indication of how

B

many they would like, and by whom exercised. They were at no time asked, beyond an inquiry made by an American commission, consisting of Messrs. Crane and King, in 1919. Nor were the results of this inquiry published. It stands to the credit of France that its Press did agitate for "la Syrie intégrale" (whole and undivided Syria), the more so since the prospects of a plebiscite would perhaps not have been too favourable to France.

We, on the other hand, have been passive in our bargain or arrangement. But it is something of a commentary upon it, that at the time we were in the midst of creating Palestinians, the Foreign Office itself published the unpalatable and contradictory truth. In Handbook No. 93, issued in 1919 under Lord Curzon by the Historical Section of that Ministry, for the guidance of diplomatists and consuls, it said, "*In modern usage the expression Palestine has no precise meaning,* but is best taken as equivalent to Southern Syria." Despite this, the Palestine Government completed a naturalisation scheme, under which there have been registered 37,997 persons with "no precise meaning."

Even political Zionists have blurted out facts about the matter. The chief organ of political Zionism in England is a pamphletic publication briefly named *Palestine*. The protagonists of political Zionism, both Jew and Christian, write and have written for it. The Zionists organisation have referred to it as one of the first examples of propaganda for their cause. In fact, it almost bursts with Zionist credentials. Well, on November 2nd, a year after the Balfour Declaration, after maintaining in one article that the French Government had got beyond considering Palestine as part of Syria, in another article—much needed—upon the boundaries of Palestine, it was obliged to state, "*Palestine has never, except for very brief periods, been a political unity,* and hardly any definition of its geographical boundaries would agree in detail."

I believe we may leave it at that, except to add that the small country of Syria is about 550 miles long and varies from 100 to 150 across. Its population is only about 3,500,000. Upon this small and now deeply impoverished country, with imports round about six times its exports, have been imposed two complete and distinct Governments, with Assemblies,

Ministers, Governors, and all the apparatus, Civil Service, and expenditure, in the manner of ancient States. To say nothing of Transjordania, the shadowy third State, where is a small native Administration.

This separation of the Syrians from themselves under the Sykes-Picot agreement was entirely theoretical at the time it was arranged, since Syria was then still in Turkish occupation. But it was not long after that we began the greatest mistake of all, one in which all the blame is ours, the patronage of, combined with service to, the Zionist scheme.

Before beginning the remarkable story of Zionist progress and of how the Balfour Declaration came into being, let me make it clear that political Zionism is one thing and Zionism another, with Judaism pure and simple even more remote. I draw from the Foreign Office's invaluable handbook a good definition of political Zionism. The Foreign Office says, " The essence of the Zionist ideal is the desire to found on the soil of Palestine a revived Hebrew nation, based on agricultural life and the use of the Hebrew language." The word that matters here is " nation."

Your political Zionist aims at establishing a Jewish nationality, a Jewish State in Palestine. The non-political Zionist wishes to return to Palestine as to the religious cradle of his creed. He seeks to create no Jewish nationality.

It is clear, of course, that if enough Jews were to emigrate to Palestine moved by this sentiment, their increasing numbers would automatically alter the political complexion of that country. But this would occur gradually, insensibly, and naturally, in the way in which immigration has altered the complexions of other countries.

The Syrians would have no cause to object to it; many have, indeed, said to me that they couldn't object. But this sort of immigration would be a slow process and the political Zionists, impatient for results in their own lifetime and forgetful that nations only settle into being through centuries of natural territorial permanence, wish for a Palestine in which their new-comers shall land, in an Irish sort of way, as residents.

They all but completely overlooked the actual residents of the country in the heat of their design. Did not a political Zionist emit for the cause this extraordinary slogan, " The people without a land for the land without a people ! " there being actually some 674,000 people in Palestine, excluding the 83,000 Jews.

These extravagant political ideas are still less shared by the ordinary Jews of the Occident. Political Zionism has brought them a measure of discredit which they do not deserve. The chief body in Anglo-Jewry, the Conjoint Committee of the Board of Deputies and the Anglo-Jewish Association, when pressed by politico-Zionists to adhere to their programme in the earlier days of the agitation, adopted a formula which was entirely equitable and correct.

It only asked the British and French Governments to secure for Jewish emigrants to Palestine their civil and religious liberties and equal political rights with the rest of the population, together with " reasonable facilities for immigration and colonisation and such municipal privileges in the towns and colonies inhabited by them as may be shown to be necessary."

One could recommend this formula to the leaders of the Syrian people when they come into their own and deal justly, as they must, with the Jews in and to be in their midst. But to politico-Zionists such a formula is and was undreamable : they wanted and want what was afterwards to be partially and insincerely defined in the Balfour Declaration as a "National Home."

The story of how the Balfour Declaration was achieved I must leave to my next article. But what marks it most was the way in which the Zionist organisers and representatives sprang from being petitioners into being wielders of power.

That something of this may be realised at once, I end by quoting textually from a most authoritative Zionist Executive report—which, though published, does not seem to have got far outside the Zionist fold, and in so far as it has got outside is forgotten—a description of the earliest stage of politico-Zionist activity and a description of the very different activity into which in a few years it developed.

This is what the report has to say of politico-Zionist work in 1914 : " Thus during the first months of the war the foundations were laid of a close understanding with the statesmen who guided the destinies of Great Britain. The time was not yet ripe for any formal assurance of support from the British Government. But an atmosphere was created in which, given favourable political conditions, it was possible to hope that such an assurance might be obtained. The friendly atmosphere was intensified during the following two years, and when Mr. Lloyd George became Prime Minister and Mr. Balfour Foreign Secretary, the seeds sown in 1914 were able to bear fruit."

BRITISH JEWS OVERRULED.

FORCING POLITICAL ZIONISM ON PALESTINE.

In 1914 Dr. Weizmann and other Zionist leaders were first introduced to Mr. Lloyd George. In 1919 the Zionist Commission was, by the avowal of a Zionist report, trying to have Sir Arthur Money, Chief Administrator of Palestine, recalled from his post. This is a big increase of power in the space of five years. But long before 1919 even political Zionism had vastly bettered its condition. You might say that it made the acquaintance of the British Government in 1914, and by 1916 was billeted upon it.

Most of those three years were given to quiet but effective spade-work. Dr. Weizmann, M. Sokoloff, Mr. Harry Sacher, and others either wrote, met Cabinet Ministers informally, or talked of Zionism to all those hundreds of people in London who count in one way or another. If you talk about a cause and write about it regularly, in the end men get accustomed to it, and are almost ready to accept it.

By the autumn of 1916 Zionism *was* accepted. "Matters had reached such a stage," says the Zionist report I quote, " that by October, 1916, the Zionist organisation felt justified in putting forward a formal statement of its views as to the future government of Palestine in the event of its coming under the control of England and France."

Need it be said that at the time it was physically impossible for any representative body from Palestine itself to put forward a formal statement of the inhabitants' views as to the future government of their own country? Most of them were under the Turks, hoping to be set free; prominent Allied sympathisers were either packed away to Asia Minor or in flight, living in Egypt or somewhere else in the Near East.

I was in the Near East myself that year, and met a number of Syrians, whose only desire was that the Allies should turn the Turks out and occupy the country. Their idea of government for Palestine was that we should govern it; the idea was pure bliss to them. They never dreamt that British occupation meant anything but British government. They were mostly in contact with our soldiers, who thought the same themselves. It never occurred to them that the destiny of Palestine was being settled by political spade-work in London.

Great numbers of them deserted from the Turkish Army last year. They are not a warlike race, and comparatively few took up arms against the Turks, but a number took great risks in the service of the Intelligence branch of our Forces. Earlier in the war several prominent citizens of Beyrut had been hanged by Jemaal Pasha, the Turkish Commander, who had discovered their correspondence with the French. The same Jemaal, flying into a temper one evening at Jaffa, cried: " I shall destroy Jaffa stone upon stone; the Jaffa people are all British."

It is but just to add that similar risks were taken and torture and death endured by members of the Aaronson family on the Phœnician coast, and that there were also Jewish fugitives in Alexandria and other places, though the latter were mainly orthodox Jews, no lovers of political Zionism.

But it was a far cry from Palestine's fugitives to London's lobbies, and, as if the fugitives never existed, out of the lobbies came the October scheme of 1916 for the government of the Holy Land.

It was a rather long document, divisible roughly under six headings; some of it unexceptionable. It held a curious clause that a Jewish Chartered Company should be established for the resettlement of Palestine by Jewish settlers. But the demand for a Jewish nation was there too. " Inasmuch as the Jewish population in Palestine forms a community with a distinct nationality and religion, it shall be officially recognised by the suzerain Government or Governments as a separate national unit or nationality." While the Chartered Company was to have power " to exercise the right of pre-emption of Crown and other lands and to acquire for its own use all or any concessions which may at any time be granted by the suzerain Government or Governments."

This is a hectoring clause, equivalent to " Hand it all over," and was accompanied by an even more hectoring passage. " The present population, being too small, too poor, and too little trained to make rapid progress, requires the introduction of a new and progressive element in the population, desirous of devoting all its energies and capital to the work of colonisation on modern lines.''

Hectoring or not hectoring, this programme appears to have been thought good enough for the British Government. '' The Government,'' says the Zionist report, '' seems to have regarded the Zionist claims embodied in the programme as forming a basis for discussion.'' Conversations with individual statesmen '' gave place to discussions of a more formal character. Zionism won recognition as one of the complex problems connected with the Middle East on the one hand and the question of small nationalities on the other.''

There you are. You could not have a better example of how the thing is done in high politics. Political Zionism under cover of being a complex problem has been put among the small nations of the Middle East. See what an advance has been made since 1914. More of an advance than you would imagine even, for the report goes on to say that this October programme '' foreshadows in its main outlines the scheme embodied in the draft Mandate for Palestine some four years later.'' In other words, *our* Mandate was based on a Zionist programme.

After this things went still more rapidly and auspiciously for the political Zionists. There was a meeting at the house of one of their number in London in February, 1917, Sir Mark Sykes being there '' in his private capacity.'' He was told that there *must* be no internationalisation of Palestine because the Zionists desired a British protectorate with full rights to the Jews to develop as a nation.

One wonders if this was the first '' must '' from the Zionists. Anyhow, M. Nahum Sokoloff, the chief representative in Britain of the International Zionist Executive, was chosen, as the result of the meeting, to continue negotiations with Sir Mark Sykes and M. Picot, who acted for the French Government. The Zionist report says with satisfaction : '' Thus opened the chapter of negotiations which ended nine months later with the Balfour Declaration.''

Still fearful of internationalisation, which would have made a Zionist State impossible, Messrs. Weizmann and Sokoloff spent some months vainly trying to get the Sykes-Picot Agreement cancelled. Though they failed in this, yet somehow internationalisation did drop out of sight.

The goal was getting visible. A number of prominent Zionists, Achad Ha-Am, the Jewish writer, Messrs. Cowen, Ettinger, Hyamson, Marks, Harry Sacher, Sieff, Leon Simon, Tolkowsky, Aaronsohn, Jabotinsky, Landman, and others from the Continental countries, as they visited England from time to time, were gathered in to form a Political Committee. Their names are of great interest, since it was they, together with the well-known Zionist leaders, who now began work on the "Balfour Declaration."

"Many different versions of the suggested formula were drafted," says the Zionist report, "by various members of the Political Committee." Drafts went back and forth to the Foreign Office. "Some were detailed and elaborate," but the Government did not want to commit itself to more than a general statement of principle. Finally, a "concise and general formula was agreed upon." This was made known to and approved by President Wilson, Sir Mark Sykes, and Baron Edmond de Rothschild. All seemed finished. On July 18th Lord Rothschild forwarded the Balfour Declaration to Mr. Balfour.

Alas! a number of British Jews, men of prominence, having no doubt had a glimpse of the proposed Declaration, sent to the Cabinet "representations antagonistic to Zionism." The Cabinet could not well proceed with the Declaration. They modified the draft and sent it to "representative Jewish leaders, both Zionist and non-Zionist." They asked for their opinions in writing. In the now submitted text the key phrase establishing Palestine as "the National Home of the Jewish people" had been changed to "a National Home for the Jewish people" in Palestine.

But Mr. Leonard Cohen, chairman of the Jewish Board of Guardians, Mr. Claude Montefiore, and Sir Philip Magnus, M.P., even now, according to the Zionist report, raised objections, "in particular to the word 'National.'" Despite their advice, in deference to the political Zionists, the British Cabinet actually retained the word "National," and with it the germ of a Jewish nationality in Syria.

They made some other modifications; then their absorption in carrying on the war and the fact that there was division of opinion in the Cabinet itself on the matter delayed publication. Something had to be done. Through Zionist influence President Wilson was brought to send " a personal message to the British Government, intimating his agreement with the idea of a pro-Zionist announcement."

This had its effect, no doubt. " Finally, all obstacles were overcome, and on November 2nd, 1917, the Foreign Secretary, Mr. Balfour, sent to Lord Rothschild the approved formula."

The Balfour Declaration was out. Not till 1920 did the British Army in Palestine deign or dare to publish it officially.

THE BALFOUR DECLARATION.
PROMISES WHICH MEAN NOTHING.

Here is the Balfour Declaration as issued on that fateful November 2nd, 1917:

> His Majesty's Government view with favour the establishment in Palestine of a National Home for the Jewish people, and will use their best endeavours to facilitate the achievement of that object, it being clearly understood that nothing shall be done which may prejudice the civil and religious rights of existing non-Jewish communities in Palestine, or the rights and political status enjoyed by the Jews in any other country.

The publication of this Declaration, as the Zionist report says, "was the signal for an unprecedented outburst of joy and enthusiasm throughout the length and breadth of Jewry." Probably "Zionist circles" would be an exacter phrase than "Jewry," but as a general statement this is, of course, substantially true. The British Government was abundantly congratulated. "Consummate act of statesmanship" and similar phrases kindled the winds that blew up Downing Street.

Only from the front of our armies in Palestine came no outburst of joy. "No official instruction seems to have been given by Whitehall in London to General Headquarters in "Cairo," says our faithful Zionist Executive report, " as to bringing their action into accord with the new idealist character which the Palestine offensive had, in view of the Balfour Declaration, acquired."

Lord Allenby was just launching this great offensive without ideals. It seems a pity that our troops, instead of being dulled by the stale worldliness of fighting for their country and blunted by the routine of redeeming the land of their Saviour, were not told of the Balfour Declaration and of how it had turned them into idealists.

But told they were not. Lord Allenby seems to have been as unidealistic as his men. "There can be no doubt," maintains the Zionist report, "but that General Allenby knew by the time that such a Declaration had been issued. But the military authorities obviously thought that any official mention of this fact in the newly conquered territory might mar the jubilation of certain sections of the population. Naturally anxious to avoid any friction which might hinder the freedom of further military operations, they preferred to abstain from any mention of the fact that the British Government had promised to support Zionist aspirations.''

Now what does this mean, put into plain English? It means that the British Government has issued a Declaration so high-handed, unwarranted, and dangerous that it was an impediment to the progress of the British Army. It had to be suppressed.

It does not matter essentially by whose orders it was suppressed. If it was suppressed by the orders of the Army, has any British Government before been censored by its own forces in the field, as if its pronouncements has been written by the enemy? If the Declaration was suppressed by order or agreement of the Government itself, how in the name of anything that is honest could the Government pretend that the issue of it was a just and straightforward act towards Palestine? It is a strange Magna Charta which cannot be published in Runnymede.

The point needs no pressing. The very fact that the Balfour Declaration was not proclaimed in Palestine till 1920 is a suffi-cient proof of its character. You have only to be a week in Palestine to learn that if agitation is to cease in that land and if it is to become in any degree a settled country making no demands, be they large or small, upon the British purse, then as a first step the Balfour Declaration ought to imitate the advice showered once upon the statesman who gave it its name. It ought to go.

It is true that Mr. Winston Churchill last year as Colonial Secretary restated the Declaration, giving what in some quarters is thought to be a new interpretation of it. But it is not a new interpretation really; I shall come to it presently. For the moment I keep to the fundamental Balfourian text. Why did the Army not publish this? Why is it the object of odium and agitation among the people of Palestine? Why ought it to be the object of both among the people of Britain? Because while it purports to represent the word of Great Britain it is a mass of phraseological tricks.

I hesitate to take you into its mazes. But it has to be done. Look and read the Declaration at the head of this article and it may seem to you a plain, honest sort of thing, in which a good deal of stress has been laid upon the protection of the Arab or Syrian population. Such indeed is the impression it was meant to convey. But examine it, as people in Palestine have examine it, and are examining it to-day, and you will open your eyes. I take four points in it.

1. What exactly is a " National Home "? Nobody knows. The expression was used because it was ambiguous. To the Syrians it is explained as a home. No man can object to the Jews having a home. To the Jews it is explained as containing the germ of Nationality, of a Jewish State.

Fifteen months after the British Government had declared that it viewed this ambiguity with favour, Mr. Lansing, the American Foreign Secretary, was obliged to ask at a meeting of the Peace Conference in Paris what " National Home " meant. Dr. Weizmann replied that it meant there should be established such conditions ultimately in Palestine that " Palestine shall be just as Jewish as America is American and England is English." Mr. (as he then was) Balfour is described as having been " very pleased " with this reply. It is difficult to see why, since Dr. Weizmann had removed with his frankness a good deal of ambiguity.

2. " Nothing shall be done," says the vigilant Declaration, " Which may prejudice the civil and religious rights of existing non-Jewish communities in Palestine." No phrase could sound better, but what exactly *are* " civil rights "? Again nobody knows. That is why the Declaration is so anxious to guarantee them. Observe that the phrase "political rights " is not used. Political rights would have been something definite. The political rights of a people are its ownership of its country. The right to have as the Syrian-Arabs demand, " a National Government created, which shall be responsible to a Parliament elected by the people of Palestine—Moslem, Christians, and Jews."

" But to grant this demand," acknowledges the foremost defender of Zionism, Mr. Israel Cohen, " would be to enable the preponderating Arab majority—Moslems and Christians—to make short work of the projected Jewish National Home." For which reason there is no mention in the Balfour Declaration of " political rights " for the preponderating majority. There is no intention of guaranteeing political rights ending in a National

Government. But in order to have the air of doing so, the vague expression " civil rights " is inserted. I asked one of the highest personages in the present Government of Palestine which was meant by " civil " rights, and he said, " Well, they are difficult to define." Precisely.

When the Zionists drew up their programme of October, 1916, the grandfather of the present mandate, did *they* ask to be guaranteed civil rights? Clause 3 of the first portion of that programme begins thus : " The Jewish population of Palestine shall enjoy full civic and *political* rights. . . " No mistake here, you see. At the end of the Balfour Declaration itself, is it civil status which is guaranteed to the Jews? Read and see. " The rights and *political* status enjoyed by the Jews." No mistake again.

Has this subterfuge passed unperceived by the whole world outside Palestine? Not quite. After the Declaration was issued the other Allied Governments were approached by the Zionist leaders to confirm it. The French communiqué they obtained was adequate but cold. But the Marchese Imperiali, then Italian Ambassador in London, in giving the Italian reply, used the Balfour formula more or less, with a sardonic addition. He said that the Government of the King of Italy " will use their best endeavours to facilitate," etc., " it being understood that this shall not prejudice the civil *and political* rights of existing non-Jewish communities." The italics are mine. The credit is Italy's.

3. This third point is less important but is worth noting. The people of Palestine are referred to as the " non-Jewish communities in Palestine." There are about 80,000 Jews and 670,000 non-Jews in Palestine. The wording would give anybody the impression that the " non-Jewish communities " were some specialised sort of bodies and not the mass of the population. Is this intended? Does Lord Balfour call the British people the " non-foreign community in England "?

4. Nothing, according to the Declaration, is to prejudice the " political status enjoyed by Jews in any other country." What does this mean? It means that Jews, besides being put on the road to establishing a Jewish State in Palestine, are also guaranteed against belonging to it if they don't wish. Political Zionists may look forward, therefore, to having their cake and eating it.

The truth peeps out very clearly from this part of the Declaration. If there existed no intention in the minds of its framers of founding a Jewish State, why were they moved to protect their co-religionists from the necessity of belonging to it? If the National Home was to be only a home, the political status of Jews elsewhere could no more be altered by it than is the status of Englishmen because thousands of them have homes in France and Italy. But if a State was erected in Palestine? Ah, then! . . . Gentlemen framers of the Balfour Declaration, what say you?

In considering these four points I have given the case against the Balfour Declaration as it is presented to-day in Palestine. It should be to the mind of anyone a most damning one. The reasons why the Army did not proclaim it till 1920 are perhaps made clear.

And now for Mr. Winston Churchill's effort to restore its character. Still trying to prove that it contains no menace to the Arabs, last year he said to the Arab delegation :

> When it is asked what is meant by the development of the Jewish National Home in Palestine, it may be answered that *it is not the imposition of a Jewish nationality upon the inhabitants of Palestine as a whole,* but the further development of the Jewish community, with the assistance of Jews in other parts of the world, in order that it may become a centre in which the Jewish people as a whole may take, on grounds of religion and race, an interest and a pride. But in order that this community should have the best prospect of free development and provide a full opportunity for the Jewish people to display its capacities, it is essential that it should know that it is in Palestine *as a right and not on sufferance.* That is the reason why it is necessary that the existence of a Jewish National Home in Palestine should be internationally guaranteed and that it should be formally recognised to rest upon ancient historic connection.
>
> This, then, is the interpretation which his Majesty's Government place upon the Declaration of 1917, and, so understood, the Secretary of State is of opinion that it does not contain or imply anything which need cause either alarm to the Arab population of Palestine or disappointment to the Jews.

Well, it is an interesting point that in Palestine few persons, outside the Zionists who complain of it, regard Mr. Churchill's restatement (which I have italicised in places) as giving any new cast to the Declaration. A high personage in Palestine said to me that this was especially regrettable. Regrettable it may be, but it is not so strange. It is Mr. Churchill's own fault.

" Mr. Churchill is no better than Lord Balfour," I was told when I talked of it in Jerusalem, "and we are more interested in the original than in the copy. To tell us, as he does, that there is no intention to impose a Jewish nationality upon the inhabitants of Palestine as a whole, and to present this as a reassuring fact, shows he has a low opinion of our intelligence.   There are old Protectorates where, in the course of time, a minority has conferred its nationality or something of the sort upon a majority.   But that a troop of brand-new immigrants should not impose its nationality and that 80,000 people should not impose their nationality upon 670,000— that is no reassurance but a thing that should follow naturally.

"And how can Mr. Churchill pretend that our rights are not menaced when he insists that the Jews do not come to Palestine on sufferance but 'as a right'? When a Russian Jew enters the Argentine, or when any immigrant enters the Argentine, or any other country, he does so on sufferance.   Englishmen go to all corners of foreign countries, out of the reach of Consuls and of England's protection, on sufferance, and make no bones about it. The word 'sufferance' sounds badly, but it is the universal condition of immigrants everywhere till such time as they become, if they so wish, naturalised by residence.   There is no stigma or wrong in sufferance, and for Mr. Churchill to pretend to see one is not worthy of a man of his calibre.

"To say that the Jews, with Hebrew as an official language, can enter Palestine on a different principle from that under which immigrants enter every other country, and at the same time to say, as Mr. Churchill has elsewhere said in his restatement, that 'the Arabic population and language is not to be subordinated' is also unworthy. There is a trick in the phrasing. If we Arabs went back to Spain 'as of right,' technically the Spaniards would not be subordinated.   If the Greek language was restored to public use in Sicily, technically the Italian language would not be subordinated. It would be on a parity. But where would the Italians be? To be put on a level of parity in your own land is not subordination, perhaps, but it is the loss of the land, the loss of the right of ruling for ever. Can Mr. Churchill deny it?"

CONTRADICTORY PLEDGES.

MISLEADING THE ARABS.

The illicit Balfour Declaration formed a platform from which all sorts of ladders were reared by the political Zionists against the walls of Jerusalem. " Its first practical outcome," says our Zionist report, " was the Zionist Commission." The terms of reference of the Commission were " to represent the Zionist organisation in Palestine and act as an advisory body to the British authorities there in all matters relating to Jews or which may affect the establishment of a National Home for the Jewish People in accordance with the Declaration of his Majesty's Government."

It was intended that this body should contain representatives of political Zionism from all countries. But the Russians could not get away because of conditions in that country, and the American Government, with a touch of humour, restrained American political Zionists from joining the Commission on the grounds that the United States were not at war with Turkey.

The French Government appointed a representative, and the Italians two, who went later to Palestine. The majority of the delegates thus came from Britain. They were Dr. Weizmann and Messrs. Joseph Cowen, Leon Simon, Eder, and Sieff.

Lord Balfour and Mr. Lloyd George " gave the Commission their unreserved support " and furnished Dr. Weizmann with letters of introduction. To the Commission as political officer was attached Mr. W. Ormsby-Gore, a member of the present Government. He has always been considered a great asset and advocate of Zionism, and certainly has pleaded its cause with vigour. But a phrase may be culled from a speech he was to make in Palestine in the June of 1918. " The Zionist movement," he was to say, *" is not merely a political move* but a spiritual force." The admission is as interesting as is the combination.

C

Dr. Weizmann was received in audience by the King before the Commission departed. It arrived in Palestine on April 4th, 1918. " Its relations with British G.H.Q. were at the beginning most cordial," says our report. Dr. Weizmann stayed with Lord Allenby. The Commission, " fully aware of the exigencies of the military situation, agreed that friction in the country might handicap operations, and that a full display of the Government's pro-Zionist attitude had better be postponed till after the victory." Nothing could be more candid.

The whole of Palestine was not captured till six months after their arrival, and while the operations continued the members of the Commission chiefly spent their time in excellent relief work amid the existing Jewish population, which had, of course, suffered from the war. The front actually ran for some time through the midst of the largest Jewish colony, Petah-Tikvah.

In the way of political results, the foundation of a Jewish university in Jerusalem was obtained, as well as authorisation for the recruiting of Palestinian Jews. The Commissioners moved about a good deal and, of course, with complete freedom; a source of annoyance to Syrians, who had not the same facilities. Rifts crept by degrees into the lute, relations between Commission and Army grew less excellent.

But in September of 1918 Dr. Weizmann was able to return to Europe with a letter from Lord Allenby to Mr. Balfour, in which Lord Allenby acknowledged Dr. Weizmann's " wise and tactful manner in the direction of the activities of the Zionist Commission," and testified to " the respect and confidence which he has inspired in all with whom he has come into contact."

It may be an opportune moment to say that, however Dr. Weizmann may have acted, he bears the reputation in Palestine of being a moderate man. How far he personally was later concerned in efforts to oust British Chief Administrators it is not possible to say. But the greater evils of political Zionism were perpetrated in Palestine while he was not there : he was always travelling. In any case, his influence was on the wane when I left that country; we shall have to deal there with strange faces and other minds.

But he may be given some benefit of doubt over the Balfour Declaration; he may not have known the British Government were breaking their word to present him with it. When it was later to be made clear that it was a bogus present he should have returned it, most surely.

Jewish units took a creditable part in the final Palestine offensive. But let it be borne in mind that amid all the talk of Jewish and Arab support the losses of both parties were trivial compared with the deaths, woundings, and sufferings which were the lot of the British troops, home or Australian, in this sector of the war.

The first were as trees planted upon the mountain of the other. Not unreasonably, therefore, the Army resented events which were to occur and showed its resentment. The Zionist report complains that the participation of Jewish troops, proclaimed in a despatch to the rest of the world, was not published in the orders of the Army of which they formed part. This was a small action, but was it smaller than the Balfour Declaration?

With Dr. Weizmann away, the rift grew between Army and Commission. The Zionist report says that within a couple of months of the defeat of the Turks the attitude of practically the entire military administration was considered by every Jew and Arab in the country as strikingly opposed to both the spirit and letter of the Balfour Declaration.

The Army " kept Jews back," " appointed two-thirds of the members of the Jerusalem Corporation Arab and only one-third Jewish, despite the Jewish majority in Jerusalem "; above all, had interfered with the position of Hebrew as a public official language. " In the summer of 1918 the Jaffa municipality had passed a law making Arabic obligatory on all signboards, and the British Military Governor had signed it. The Zionist Commission intervened and the by-law was quashed." (Is it necessary to state that Arabic is the language of most of the people of Jaffa?)

" But after the victory the blow came straight from the Jerusalem Headquarters. The Chief Administrator (Major-General Money) decided that all tax forms and tax receipts should be printed in English and Arabic alone."

This sort of legislation was intolerable to Zionists. Their report says : " It is most unfair to say that the Palestine Jews were hasty, impatient, and expected a Jewish ' Government ' to be established at once and ready made. . . . They never expected either a Jewish Government or an artificial Jewish predominance. But they *did* expect a *sympathetic* Government and, above all, a strict adherence to the principle of equality of rights granted to all races and languages under British rule." These protestations only require to be examined.

If a minority of 1 in 8 can fix language laws, what else in the world does it own but an artificial predominance? What is there but a Jewish Government? Nor does British rule confer equality of rights to all languages or anything of the sort. You would think that the King had sworn it upon his throne, the way it is put, but there are no such fixed regulations. We work in this matter, as we have always done with success, by rule of thumb. Where there are diversities of tongue in the British Empire, their public use is determined by their practical value.

To follow the opposite course, as has now been done in Palestine, is to produce what happens in the Advisory Council in Jerusalem, where a member speaks in English, which has to be translated into Arabic and then Hebrew, and then a member speaks in Arabic, which has to be put into English and Hebrew, and then a member speaks in Hebrew, which goes into Arabic and English. Business is, shall we say, retarded. In addition to constructing a National Home we are building a small Babel.

So after all General Money in his days was only aiming at a little more common-sense rule and a little less chaos. However, his " blow straight from the Headquarters " was to be reduced to the level of a mere graze in comparison with the blow that was soon delivered. It was November, 1918, and everywhere where there were lesser peoples under enemy rule the Allies were assuring them of their support in a formal fashion. The Arabs could not be left out. The Army authorities were determined they should not be left out, and so, with their interest in North Syria, were the French. What the attitude of our Government was it is impossible for any man to understand. As far as I can see, they had a lapse into integrity. But was it voluntary? In any case the following joint Anglo-French proclamation was published throughout Syria with full formality. Read it now, you who have read the Declaration of all the Balfours, and again when you have a little time to spare for wonder :

" The end that France and Great Britain have in pursuing in the East the war unloosed by German ambition is the complete and definite freeing of the peoples so long oppressed by the Turks, and *the establishment of national Governments and Administrations deriving their authority from the initiative and free choice of the indigenous populations.*

" In order to give effect to these intentions, France and Great Britain have agreed to encourage and assist the establishment of indigenous Governments and Administrations in Syria and Mesopotamia, now freed by the Allies, and in the territories whose liberation they seek, and to recognise them as soon as they are effectively established.

" Far from wishing to impose any particular institutions on the populations of these regions, their only care is to assure by their support and efficacious assistance the normal working of the Governments *which they shall have freely given themselves.* To assure impartial and equal justice for all, to facilitate the economic development of the country by promoting and encouraging local initiative, to foster the spread of education, to put an end to the divisions too long exploited by Turkish policy—such is the rôle which the two Allied Governments claim in the liberated territories."

The British Government did not push its claim, did it? What is to be said of a Government which spoke in such solemn tones, engaging the credit of every British subject, and yet had issued the Balfour Declaration and was treating even then with political Zionists " as of right " in Whitehall? If the Government had been an individual, a judge of the High Court would have sent the papers to the Public Prosecutor.

BROKEN FAITH WITH THE ARABS.

McMAHON LETTERS DISCLOSURES.

You have seen how the Declaration of all the Balfours was composed and how the British Army in Palestine for over two years did not publish it, and what happened in Palestine as a result. Now let us descend into the real depths and watch how the British Government originally broke its word.

It did so by publishing that Declaration at all. It had given pledges to the Arabs previously guaranteeing the independence of the country in which it now sought to establish the Zionist " National Home." So that the " National Home " was preceded and followed by broken pledges; this pledge and the Anglo-French pledge of 1918.

These pledges are contained in the letters which were sent to the Shereef of Mecca (now King Hussein of the Hedjaz) by Sir Henry McMahon, when the entry of the Arabs into the war on our side against the Turks was negotiated. Sir Henry McMahon was High Commissioner in Egypt at the time, and was acting in the name of Great Britain.

The McMahon letters were never published by the late Government. They are State Papers, and as such were by Government regulations not to be divulged. In this matter the Government kept faith with itself, at least. The correspondence is long, and within the limits of a newspaper it is not possible to publish it all. I shall quote the relevant portions.

It should be understood that the Shereef Hussein was acting on behalf of the Arab people. It will be seen he was a good bargainer and, indeed, the Arabs were no less anxious to be subsidised by Britain than they were to be set free by Britain. But if he bargained, we made an agreement and are obliged to keep it, having drawn or intended to draw our own advantages from it. The Shereef stood out for his boundaries from the start,

and was well advised, in view of the Balfour Declaration men-
tality of our Government.

On July 14th, 1915, the Shereef sent a formal letter to Sir
Henry McMahon, declaring :

> Whereas the whole of the Arab nation without any exception has decided
> in these last years to live, and to accomplish their freedom and grasp
> the reins of their administration both in theory and practice . . . for
> these reasons the Arab nation sees fit to limit itself, as time is short, to
> asking the Government of Great Britain, if it should think fit, for the
> approval through its deputy or representative of the following fundamental
> propositions . . . until such time as it finds occasion for making the
> actual negotiations :—
>
> Firstly, Great Britain will acknowledge the independence of the Arab
> countries, in every sense of the word independence, to be bounded on the
> north by Mersina-Adana up to the 37th degree of latitude, on which degree
> falls Biridjik, Ourfa, Mardin, Midiat, Amadia Island, up to the borders
> of Persia. On the east by the frontiers of Persia up to the Gulf of Basra
> On the south by the Indian Ocean, with the exception of the colony of
> Aden, which is excepted from these boundaries. On the west by the
> Red Sea and *the Mediterranean Sea up to Mersina*.

There were several other clauses, giving us economic priority,
guaranteeing the Arab State material and moral aid against
attacks from within or without, defining attitude in case of either
party entering upon aggressive action, securing supply of funds
and munitions to the Arabs, fixing the duration of the proposed
treaty between Britain and the Arabs to fifteen years, and others
again.   But what matters in this present report is the first clause,
since it contains the boundaries of the proposed Arab State.

On August 30th Sir Henry McMahon replied :

> We have the honour to thank you for your frank expression of the
> sincerity of your feeling towards England. We rejoice that your Highness
> and your men are of one opinion that Arab interests are British interests
> and British Arab. And in this intent we confirm to you the terms of
> Lord Kitchener's message, which reached you by the hand of —— (a
> certain Arab gentleman) . . . in which our desire for the independence
> of the Arabs and the Arab countries . .   has been stated.   . . As
> regards the question of boundaries, it would appear to be premature to
> consume our time in discussing such details in the heat of war and while
> in many portions of them the Turk is up till now in effective occupation :
> especially as we have learned to our surprise and regret that some of the
> Arabs in these very parts, far from assisting us, are neglecting this, their
> supreme opportunity, and are lending their arms to the German and the
> Turk, to the new despoiler and the old oppressor. . . .

The Shereef Hussein was much too practised and shrewd to be
moved by these considerations.   He replied on September 9th to
" His Excellency the Most Exalted, the most Eminent the British
High Commissioner in Egypt; may God grant his success " :

> ' . . It is necessary to make clear to your Excellency our sincerity
> towards the illustrious British Empire and our. confession of preference
> for it in all cases and matters and under all forms and circumstances. .

Nevertheless, your Excellency will pardon me and permit to say clearly that the coldness and hesitation which you have displayed in the question of the limits and boundaries by saying that the discussion of these at present is of no use and is a loss of time, etc.,   might be taken to infer an estrangement or something of the sort.

In lengthy Oriental phrases the Shereef stuck out for his boundaries, and said that if any Arabs were still under Turco-German orders it was only because of the delay in the present negotiations.

In reply he received from Sir Henry McMahon a communication of the utmost importance, dated October 25th.

" I regret," said Sir Henry McMahon, " that you should have received from my last letter the impression that I regarded the question of the boundaries with coldness and hesitation. This was not the case, but it appeared to me that the moment had not yet arrived when they could be most profitably discussed.

" However, from your last letter I realised that you regard this question to be of vital and urgent importance, and have therefore lost no time in informing the Government of Great Britain of the contents of your letter, and it is with great pleasure that I communicate to you on their behalf the following statement which I am confident you will receive with satisfaction :

" 1. The districts of Mersina and Alexandretta and *portions of Syria lying to the west of the districts of Damascus, Homs, Hama, and Aleppo* cannot be said to be purely Arab and should therefore be excluded from the desired boundaries.

" 2. *With these modifications*, and without prejudice to certain treaties enacted between ourselves and some Arabian chiefs, *we accept these boundaries*.

" And as regards those portions of the territories therein in which Great Britain is free to act without detriment to the interests of her Ally, France, I am empowered in the name of the Government of Great Britain to enter into the following covenant (the Arabic word is *mawathik*) and reply to your letter as under :—

" 1. *Subject to the above modifications, Great Britain is prepared to recognise and support the independence of the Arabs within the territories included in the limits and boundaries proposed by the Shereef of Mecca.*

" 2. Great Britain guarantees the safety of the Holy Places against any foreign aggression and will recognise their individuality.

" 3. When the situation admits, Great Britain will give the Arabs her advice and will assist them to establish what may appear to be the most suitable forms of government in these various territories.

" 4. On the other hand, it is understood that the Arabs have decided to seek the advice and guidance of Great Britain only, and that such European advisers and officials as may be required for the formation of a sound form of administration will be British.

" 5. With regard to the Vilayets (provinces) of Baghdad and Basra, the Arabs will recognise that the established position and interests of Great Britain necessitate special measures of administrative control in order to secure these territories from foreign aggression, to promote the welfare of the local populations, and to safeguard our mutual economic interests."

To this Sir Henry McMahon added that if there were minor points an opportunity for discussing them might be found later; he had kept to the essentials.

On November 5th the Shereef replied accepting.   He said:

> In order to facilitate an agreement and render a service to Islam . . .
> we renounce our insistence on the inclusion of the Vilayet of Mersina
> and Adana in the Arab kingdom. *But the provinces of Aleppo and Beyrout
> and their sea coasts are purely Arab provinces,* and there is no difference
> between a Moslem and a Christian Arab (there are many Christians in
> these districts) ; they are descendants of one forefather.

Five clauses followed, dealing with Irak and the position of
Arabia in face of Turkey.   The letter ended:

> We know that our lot in this war will be either a success which will
> guarantee to the Arabs a life becoming their past history or destruction
> in the attempt to obtain their objects.   Were it not for the determination
> I see in the Arabs to attain these objects, I should have preferred to seclude
> myself upon a mountain height ; but they, the Arabs, have insisted that
> I should guide the movement to this end.   May God keep you safe and
> victorious, as we devoutly hope and desire.

The accord was almost at hand.   Sir Henry McMahon wrote
on December 14th :

> I am gratified to observe that you agree to the exclusion of the Vilayet
> of Mersina and Adana (Alexandretta is in this district) from the boundaries
> of the Arab territories. . . . *With regard to the Vilayets of Aleppo and
> Beyrout,* the Government of Great Britain has taken careful note of your
> observations, but as *the interests of our Ally France are involved, the
> question will require careful consideration,* and a further communication
> on the subject will be addressed to you in due course.

On New Year's Day, 1916, the Shereef penned his final letter
to the " excellent, energetic and magnanimous Minister."   He
made his position upon the Syrian districts clear :

> *As regards the northern parts* and their coasts we have already stated
> in our previous letter what were the utmost possible modifications, and
> all this was only done so as to fulfil those aspirations whose attainment
> is desired by the will of the Blessed and Supreme God.   It is the same
> feeling and desire which impelled us to avoid what may possibly injure
> the alliance of Great Britain and France and the agreement made between
> them in the present war and calamities ; yet we find it our duty that the
> Eminent Minister should be sure that at the first opportunity after this
> war is finished *we shall ask you (which we now avert our eyes from to-day)
> for what we now leave to France at Beyrout and on its coasts.*

The Government, satisfied with this shelving, gave Sir Henry
McMahon final instructions, and he was able to tell the Shereef,
" I have received orders from my Government to inform you that
all your demands are accepted, and that all you ask for will be
sent (presumably money and munitions)."

Such is the McMahon correspondence.   The pledges in it were
formally confirmed in 1918, when the Turks tried to get the
Arabs to enter into a separate treaty with them on the understanding that Turkey would recognise the independence of the
Arab countries.   King Hussein cabled the news of this offer to
the British Government.   Our Foreign Minister, then Mr.

Balfour, replied through the British representative at Jeddah, thanking King Hussein for the loyal information, and declaring : " His Britannic Majesty's Government, in agreement with the Allied Powers, confirms its previous pledges respecting the recognition of the independence of the Arab countries.''

In my next article it will be my task to show how deeply these letters pledge us, how the establishment of a Jewish National Home breaks them, and how, realising this, Mr. Churchill last year made a disastrous effort to show they had never been given, and, failing in this, threw them into the waste-paper basket of the Colonial Office.

MR. CHURCHILL INVENTS A PROVINCE.
PLEDGE IN WASTE-PAPER BASKET.

On the pledges contained in the McMahon correspondence, given at length in my last article but never published by the recent Government, the Palestine delegates, who were here last year and who again a few weeks ago returned to London, base their demand for the revocation of the Balfour Declaration.

They do not base it on this correspondence alone, since they can also base it on the Anglo-French proclamation of November, 1918, and since they can still more base it on natural rights. But they claim that in addition here is Great Britain, in the person of Sir Henry McMahon, pledging the independence of Palestine to the Arab people in the person of the then Shereef of Mecca. They claim that this pledge was as solemnly renewed, as it was solemnly given in the first place, by Mr. Balfour in his cable to King Hussein in 1918.

They claim that it was a breach of faith for the British Government, having guaranteed Palestine as an independent State, subsequently to guarantee within it a " Jewish National Home," and they maintain with an exactness which cannot be questioned that such subsequent guarantee is null and void and that the Balfour Declaration has and has had absolutely no value nor binding force whatsoever, formerly, now or hereafter.

The claim is luminous in its simplicity. In the Shereef's letter he proposes among the boundaries of the Arab kingdom, independent in every sense of the word independent, the Persian frontier on the east and the Mediterranean on the west. *Within these limits lies Palestine.* Sir Henry McMahon in his second letter says, " *We accept these boundaries with modifications.*"

Could anything be clearer? Unless Palestine falls within the sphere of the modifications, all is up with the Declaration of all the Balfours and the legitimacy from any point of view of the " National Home." There is and can be no bias in this statement.

I ask any Jewish reader to consider what was the attitude towards his people of a Government which could ceremoniously offer them forged title-deeds.

Now the modifications with equal clarity specify that " *portions of Syria lying to the west of the districts of Damascus, Homs, Hama, and Aleppo* cannot be said to be purely Arab and therefore should be excluded " from the Arab boundaries. Get an atlas of your own out, if you like, to find what are these portions of Syria. It is as easy as possible. Find Damascus first: it is the key place. There it is in the centre of Syria; roughly speaking, the French mandatory area is north, the British south. The French overlaps a little. Where is the next place, now, Homs? North. Where is Hama? North again. Where is Aleppo? Northernmost of all. The four towns form a line, as it were, on the desert's edge. What are the excluded portions lying west of them? Approximately it is the country facing Cyprus, comprising the towns of Sidon, Beyrout, Tripoli, Latakia, Antioch as we go up towards Alexandretta, Mersina, and the rest of the excluded land.

Where does Palestine lie? Where are Haifa, Nablus, Jaffa, Jerusalem, the cities and towns of Palestine? South, south, far to the south. The decisive line that went westward from Damascus struck the coast between Tyre and Sidon. (As a matter of fact, the Anglo-Palestino-Franco-Syrian boundary of to-day is not so far off, at a place named Ras-el-Nakoora.) Below it, safe from exclusion, are the cities of Palestine, 60, 80, 120 miles below.

Besides, does not Sir Henry McMahon only speak of reconsideration where the " interests of France are interwoven " ? And the Shereef Hussein in his final letter, has he anything more to ask for but " *the northern parts* and their coasts. . . . now left to France "? And " France " stops some 15 miles below Tyre. All that is south goes, by the word of Sir Henry McMahon, which is the word of Great Britain, to form an independent kingdom for the Arabs.

And yet our Cabinet could impose a " Jewish National Home " within these boundaries to the conservation of which it was pledged !

Did that Cabinet put forward no defence of its action? Better by far for that Cabinet if it had never done so. But through the mouth of Mr. Winston Churchill it did. Listen to him :

" This promise to recognise the independence of the Arabs was given subject to a reservation made in the same letter, which excluded from its scope the country lying to the west of the vilayet (province) of Damascus."

The then Colonial Secretary added that since this vilayet included the whole of Transjordania, therefore the portions to the west of it, the excluded portions, covered Palestine as it now is. That is to say, he paid no attention to the names of Homs, Hama, and Aleppo, in the McMahon text, the line of towns going *north* from Damascus, but produced as from a conjurer's tall hat a line going *south* from Damascus which satisfied his requirements.

Now, if this Churchillian line were genuine the whole of Syria would have been excluded, since Homs, Hama, and Aleppo would have excluded the northern part. It stands to reason that if the British high contracting parties had meant to exclude all Syria they would have specified " Syria." The phraseology imputed by Mr. Churchill to himself and his colleagues is preposterous.

If you or I or any ordinary man in his senses wished to exclude England from some convention, should we say, " We exclude the country lying to the west of the districts of Dover, London, Ipswich, Skegness, Hull, Sunderland, and Berwick " ? Of course not; we should say, " We exclude England."

But there is worse than this to come—far worse. In order to give a show of fact to his plea, Mr. Churchill spoke of " the vilayet of Damascus." The vilayets or provinces of Syria were those of Aleppo, Beyrout, and Suriya (our word Syria is a corruption of this). Deir-ez-Zor, the Lebanon, and Jerusalem were self-sufficing sanjaks or counties outside the vilayets; the Lebanon had a special autonomous régime. These were the only divisions of the country. *There is no vilayet of Damascus; it does not exist !*

Naturally, it is not to be found in the McMahon text; if you read you will see the word used is " district " (*moukataa* in the Arabic). As in English, it is a word of loose general meaning, with the sense of the immediate surroundings of a city. Whereas, by speaking of a supposed vilayet or province, Mr. Churchill could make it stretch far south, and exclude any desired stretches of territory that got in its way. The Palestine delegates icily pointed out to him the inexistence of the " vilayet of Damascus."

A pretty position for a British Minister. He had invented a province and invented a territory. It was in vain. He was proved wrong. The pledge stood. Now comes what I regret to have to recall. It may well have been that when Mr. Churchill made his reply he had depended upon geographical information drawn from an official of his Ministry who had made a mistake. Ministers and officials are human and make such mistakes.

But, when the errors are discovered, what do they do? We have been prone to think that they honourably repair them and revoke any action founded upon the error. Did Mr. Churchill set about redeeming the British pledge? Listen to his astonishing reply to the Syrian Delegation.

" The comments you were good enough to offer (i.e., " There is no vilayet of Damascus ") . . . were carefully considered by the Secretary of State, who, after consulting the authorities concerned with the early correspondence between Sir Henry McMahon and the King of the Hedjaz " (i.e., after consulting Sir Henry McMahon) *" decided to make a modification in the draft on a point of fact."* The Syrians were proved right, so Mr. Churchill altered a word or so in his draft reply to them. No more.

Please understand what this means. The Secretary of State took up his reply to the Syrian Arabs, crossed out his own vilayet, " the vilayet of Churchill " put in " District of Damascus," left out " Homs, Hama, and Aleppo," added " this district has always been regarded as covering the vilayet of Beyrout and the independent sanjak of Jerusalem." Where was the recognition of the proved pledge? There was none. Where was the pledge? It had gone into the waste-paper basket. It had been suppressed. Unable to disprove it, the British Minister says, " it has always been regarded " as what it is not, and for him that closes the affair.

And the word and honour of England, built up so painfully and lengthily by generations of Civil Servants and soldiers and merchants who have always in all parts of the globe kept their word? In the waste-paper basket, too.

WHEEDLING THE PEACE CONFERENCE.

EXTREME CLAIMS BY THE ZIONISTS.

The British Government having announced in November, 1918, by public proclamation through Syria its intention of establishing "national Governments and Administrations deriving their authority from the initiative and free choice of the indigenous populations," said to itself, in so far as a Government can, " So that's that," and resumed its intercourse with the political Zionists in London.

Dr. Weizmann met Mr. Balfour again, who told him that the Zionists " would probably be heard at the Peace Conference when the national problem with which they were concerned came up, and that Great Britain was pledged to the policy of a National Home and would therefore support it at the Conference."　Mr. Balfour was correct on all points except that there was no national problem in Palestine, that Great Britain was pledged to the Arabs, and that therefore it could not support the Zionists at the Conference.

The power of the Zionist Organisation was growing. Jews throughout the world perceived this and began to come to the politico-Zionists for help in all sorts of matters which affected them. The aim of the politico-Zionists was being effected; they were growing into a Government. " In many cases the organisation, by now in a position of some influence in Government circles, made successful representations at the Foreign Office." If the Foreign Office allowed the organisation to act for the subjects of Powers having Ambassadors or Ministers at the Court of St. James's, it is not to be congratulated. In fact, there were so many calls of this sort upon the organisation that it made an arrangement with another body, the Committee of Jewish Delegations (which had been established to press the claims of Jewish minorities in East European countries), to take over the work, and restricted itself to matters " more directly connected with Palestine."

Preparations for the Peace Conference were hurried on. Drafts of proposals were sent to the Foreign Office, which by now must have had a fine collection of Zionist drafts. Jewish conferences sent in resolutions in favour of British trusteeship, and a Jewish " Commonwealth " in Palestine. " Commonwealth " was bound to arrive sooner or later in the politico-Zionist text-book : it is just the sort of word to suit with all the power it confers hidden under its friendly society sort of sound. It reappeared in the formal statement of the Zionist Organisation regarding Palestine which was presented to the Peace Conference in February, 1919.

This was a very long document indeed. It developed the " Historic Title of the Jews to Palestine "; fixed the boundaries of the country, enumerated proposals for the Mandate, for the establishment of a Land Commission, for the formation of a Jewish Council in Palestine to represent the Jews, for the recognition of Hebrew as a public language, for naturalisation, for everything, in fine, that appertains to the life and government of a country.

It proposed that the sovereign possession of Palestine " shall be vested in the League of Nations and the government entrusted to Great Britain as Mandatory of the League," but the Mandate was to be subject to the following special conditions :—

> Palestine shall be placed under such political, administrative, and economic conditions as will secure the establishment there of the Jewish National Home and ultimately render possible *the creation of an autonomous Commonwealth*, it being clearly understood, etc. (The clause ended with the finish of the Balfour Declaration.)

The tone of this, the third of the great Zionist programmes which were to form the basis for the present Mandate and Constitution of Palestine, is superior to that of its predecessors, however unreasonable be its existence. It is possible to trace in it a moderating hand. Its signatories were Lord Rothschild; on behalf of the Zionist Organisation, Dr. Chaim Weizmann and M. Nahum Sokoloff; on behalf of the Zionist Organisation of America, Messrs. Julian W. Mack, Stephen S. Wise, Harry Friedenwald, Jacob de Haas, Louis Robison, Bernard Flexner, and Mary Fels (widow of the soap-maker); on behalf of the Russian Zionist Organisation, Israel Rosoff; on behalf of the Jewish population of Palestine " in accordance with mandate received," Messrs. Weizmann and Sokoloff again.

The next step was the celebrated hearing of the Zionist delegates by the members of the Peace Conference. There was a significant start to this meeting. The Zionist report says, " The Conference started at 3.30. M. Clemenceau left in a few minutes." That unambiguous man ! In the course of the Conference Dr. Weizmann made his memorable statement about Palestine being as Jewish as England is English and America American. Mr. Lansing put his memorable question, " What is meant by a Jewish National Home"?

A certain amount of excitement was created in Paris. The Emir Feisul, who was there at the time, made hot and cold statements about the National Home. The political Zionists themselves know that statements extorted from that charming, much-prompted prince, did nothing but injure him and to them were valueless. His position on the morrow of the various declarations he was obliged to make must, as he read them, have been rather like that of Lord Balfour himself, who, presented by a secretary one morning of the same Peace Conference with a shorthand draft of a statement he had made the day before, read it through with an air of detached analysis, asked after some time, " Am I to understand that I said this yesterday ? " was assured that he had indeed done so, and finally declared, " I wish it clearly to be appreciated that these words do not represent the opinion of His Majesty's Government," and after a pause, " nor, indeed, do they represent my own." The world still awaits Lord Balfour's unprejudiced opinion of the Balfour Declaration.

The Zionist report shows us next that someone in London had begun to take fright at the position in which the Government had placed itself. The politico-Zionist leaders were told that such phrases as " Jewish Palestine " and even the homely " Jewish Commonwealth " were premature. Dr. Weizmann when he spoke of a Jewish Palestine spoke out honestly at least. But our Government did not want this sort of talk.

Meanwhile, what was happening in Palestine? Terrible things. What a change of atmosphere ! The report is almost tearful. " Late in October, 1919, the Military Governor of Jaffa, in reply to a letter addressed to him by the Moslem-Christian Club, stated in writing that the Balfour Declaration simply meant that

D

Jews should be allowed to come to Palestine in the same way as any other individuals. The letter was circulated to all Arab clubs in the country as well as to certain foreign Consuls. Whether the Governor acted under instructions or under his own initiative is uncertain.'' Perhaps the Governor had been reading the British proclamation about "Administrations deriving their authority from the initiative and free choice of the indigenous populations.'' There is a dull straightforwardness about soldiers, a thick adhesiveness to the letter of the law.

The *new* Governor of Jaffa in the autumn (there is something suspicious about that word "new" to my mind), Lieutenant-Colonel Hubbard, does not seem to have been much of an improvement. He declared he was going to address Jewish delegations in Arabic.

"In order to avoid a scandal the Zionist Commission reported this conversation to Jerusalem the same night, and General Money sent the zealous Governor an order to abstain from such pro-Arab manifestations.'' The Zionist Executive report continues to pile up evidence of this kind against our Army. General Money and Lord Allenby are treated with extreme insolence. "A striking outward manifestation of this (anti-Jewish) atitude was given by General Money himself at a concert in a Jewish school, where the Chief Administrator and his staff kept their seats while the 'Hattikva' was being played. The Jewish National Anthem was well known to every Englishman in the country *even* General Allenby, only six months before, at the Mount Scopus celebration, had risen and stood to attention while the 'Hattikva' was being sung. General Money's demonstration was a clear sign of a change for the worse.'' This is a report of the supreme body of Zionism, mark you. "*Even* General Allenby.''

It was very difficult to make Whitehall appreciate all this. "In London the political atmosphere was very different; the position of Zionism in all influential circles and the personal authority of Zionist leaders was very strong. It seemed psychologically impossible to reconcile the melancholy reports from Palestine with *the cloudless benevolence pervading every Government office in London.*

Yet the impossible was done. "In this connection Mr. Louis Brandeis's visit to Palestine in July, 1919, was of great assistance. Short though his stay was, it enabled him to get an unbiased view of the situation and to report on it after his return to England. Soon afterwards Major-General Money was replaced as Chief Administrator by Major-General Watson, and some of the crudest infringements of the principle of equality—especially with regard to the position of the Hebrew language—were removed." Mr. Louis Brandeis is one of the most distinguished judges of the U.S. Supreme Court, and at present his influence in Palestine is being cast on the side of sanity. But if Lord Coleridge, say, visited Washington after a short but unbiased stay in Hawaii and reported, etc., and some crude American infringement shortly after left Hawaii, what would the American people have to say, I wonder?

Nineteen hundred and nineteen and 1920 were passed by the politico-Zionist leaders in London and other European capitals in an endeavour to have the frontiers of Palestine fixed according to their Peace Conference proposals. They wished particularly to be included in "Palestine" the sources of the Jordan, the headwaters and tributaries of the Yarmook, and a right of access to the waters of the Litany.

Lord Allenby's support was won "from the military standpoint." Sir Herbert Samuel, shortly to be appointed High Commissioner in Palestine, who had helped the Zionists in many ways for some years, used his influence. The American Ambassador was instructed to make representations. "Canadian and South African and Australian Zionists were successful in inducing their respective Prime Ministers to cable to the British Government in support of the Zionist boundary." But all to little avail. If Britain had to think of "Palestine," France thought of "Syria," and the Franco-British Convention of December 23rd, 1920, had to ratify the present frontiers.

ZIONIST DICTATORS.

AN INTOLERABLE SITUATION.

There is a very different side to the picture of Mr. Lloyd George in San Remo telling Zionist leaders, as he did, that what was wanted in Palestine were men who cared for the National Home policy, and of the Zionist Executive, superciliously secure with a disingenuous British Government reporting that a British official " can only succeed in Palestine under the Mandate if he be a sincere and convinced friend of Zionist aspirations." The other side was in Palestine itself.

While the strings were being spun that were to be pulled in San Remo, the Chief Administrator of Palestine, Sir Louis Bols, K.C.B., had sent to General Headquarters in Cairo a despatch upon the riots in Jerusalem.

> " I cannot allocate the blame," he says fairly, " to any section of the community or to individuals while their case is still *sub judice*, but I can definitely state that when the strain came the Zionist Commission did not loyally accept the orders of the Administration, but from the commencement adopted a hostile, critical, and abusive attitude. It is a regrettable fact that, with one or two exceptions, it appears impossible to convince a Zionist of British good faith and ordinary honesty.
>
> " They seek, not justice from the military occupant, but that in every question in which a Jew is interested discrimination in his favour shall be shown. They are exceedingly difficult to deal with. In Jerusalem, being in the majority, they are not satisfied with military protection, but demand to take the law into their own hands ; in other places where they are in a minority they clamour for military protection."

On April 9th the Chief Administrator had received a letter in a most overbearing strain from Messrs. Ussishkin and Yellin, the former the chief of the Russian Zionists and still a member of the Zionist Executive, the latter a prominent political Zionist and till recently the president of the National Council of Jews in Palestine. They spoke of the riots as if Jerusalem was in the throes of a Bartholomew massacre, said Sir Louis Bols had insulted them and their community by not receiving them when they called, told him he had broken his promises, and that police were taking part in the riots.

Then they delivered an ultimatum :

> We find it our sacred duty to declare to you that the Jewish population both young and old, have *decided that within two hours*, if their safety is not completely assured and their protection fully guaranteed, they will find themselves forced to realise that they cannot leave their fate in the hands of others, and will, as one man, rise to defend themselves and their brothers who are being maltreated and murdered before their eyes.

The responsibility, they declared, would fall on the Chief Administrator.

The latter had already seen Dr. Weizmann on the 5th to concert the measures for Jewish safety. They had talked at length; Sir Louis Bols had sent his Chief of Staff with Dr. Weizmann to see the Military Governor, and from there he had been taken on to the headquarters of the 8th Division. The total losses in the riots were six Jews and six Arabs.

> " It is unnecessary to press my difficulty," comments Sir Louis Bols, " in controlling any situation that may arise in the future if I have to deal with a representative of the Jewish community (M. Ussishkin was vice-president) who threatens me with mob law and refuses to accept the constituted forces of law and order."

The Zionist Commission acted, in fact, as if it was the lord of Palestine. The Chief Administrator complains of the " peremptory and dictatorial tone of letters from the Zionist Commission. I had to tell the Zionist Commission in the matter of a letter sent to the Governor of Gaza that I would not tolerate such letters to my subordinates, and that any complaints must be made to me."

Continuing his despatch, which I am fortunate in being able to publish so that the public may learn what a régime the British Cabinet knowingly was backing, the Chief Administrator cites an astounding letter sent directly to one of his officers. Let me quote it verbatim :

> To Lieutenant Howes, A.D.A.A.P.,
>   Military Governorate, Jerusalem.
>
> Our attention has been drawn to the fact that of late several Jewish candidates for the gendarmerie have been accepted without recommendation from or reference to this Commission
> We take the liberty to point out that *it is the wish of the Zionist Commission that all candidates should pass through their hands ; their credentials should be scrutinised by us so that we may be certain that only the right men are finally presented to you for acceptance.* Only by this method can

the Zionist Commission be able to exercise an indirect control and be in any way responsible for the efficiency of the Jewish gendarmes.

We feel certain that you will appreciate the validity of this argument and express your agreement with the desirability of the principle we submit—namely, that no Jewish candidate be accepted who does not bear a recommendation from this Commission.

MAX NUROCK,
Secretary of the Zionist Commission.

23-2-20.

At the present moment Mr. Max Nurock is Junior Assistant Civil Secretary in Government House, Jerusalem. That a letter of this sort should be sent to a British officer in any case, and that into the bargain it should be sent over his superiors' heads, shows to what a size the arrogance had grown which was fed on the easy pledge-breaking of the Companions of Honour in Whitehall. Sir Louis Bols had inquiries made and there appeared to be no escape from this procedure. He states, " Many excellent Jewish recruits, Palestinians of the best type, object to the authority of the Zionist Commission in this matter and have thereby been lost to the force."

The Chief Administrator passed to an example of fraud. " The Zionist Commission have a very complete Criminal Investigation Department of their own, and many of their reports have been of use to the Administration. But again this dual control is liable to abuse, one of their agents having been arrested a short time ago in Hebron in possession of a pass issued by a Zionist Commission secret agent. This pass certified the bearer to be on the C.I.D. of Occupied Enemy Territory Administration (South) duty."

Sir Louis Bols continued his despatch, which was indeed an indictment, by retailing how immigrants disappeared into nowhere and how unwearied efforts on the part of the Administration and requests to the Zionist Commission for assistance had failed to obtain him the whereabouts of 10 per cent. of a shipload of (suspicious) immigrants who had given their address as Jaffa. The Commission had sent forty-eight immigrants to Jerusalem after only two days' out of a fixed five days' quarantine. These had come from plague, typhus, and small-pox infected ports. The Zionist judicial system, complete with courts and penalties, usurped the privileges of the Government. Zionist medical units, despite good work, resisted serving under the control of the Public Health Department. Violent attacks were permitted by the

Zionist Organisation in the Hebrew Press upon schools where English was the language of instruction.

The Chief Administrator gave these as examples of what was constantly occurring and formally concluded his despatch as follows·:

> It will be recognised from the foregoing that my own authority and that of every department of my Administration is claimed or impinged upon by the Zionist Commission, and I am definitely of opinion that this state of affairs cannot continue without grave danger to the public peace and to the prejudice of my Administration.
>
> It is no use saying to the Moslem and Christian elements of the population that our declaration as to the maintenance of the status quo made on our entry into Jerusalem has been observed. Facts witness otherwise: the introduction of the Hebrew tongue as an official language; the setting up of a Jewish judicature; the whole fabric of government of the Zionist Commission of which they are well aware); the special travelling privileges to members of the Zionist Commission: this has firmly and absolutely convinced the non-Jewish elements of our partiality. On the other hand the Zionist Commission accuse my officers and me of anti-Zionism. The situation is intolerable and in justice to my officers and myself must be firmly faced.
>
> This Administration has loyally carried out the wishes of his Majesty's Government and has succeeded in so doing by strict adherence to the laws governing the conduct of the Military Occupant of Enemy Territory, but this has not satisfied the Zionists, who appear bent on committing the temporary military administration to a partialist policy before the issue of the Mandate. *It is manifestly impossible to please partisans who officially claim nothing more than a " National Home," but in reality will be satisfied with nothing less than a Jewish State and all that it politically implies.*
>
> *I recommend, therefore, in the interests of peace, of development, of the Zionists themselves, that the Zionist Commission in Palestine be abolished.*

Of course, this being the recommendation of the head of the British Administration, was not acted upon by the British Government. " What you want, Weizmann, in Palestine are men who really *care* for the policy of the National Home," said Mr. Lloyd George.

THE MANDATE PUZZLE.

CIVIL GOVERNMENT INSTALLED.

On June 30th, 1920, Sir Louis Bols departed and the Military Administration was " brought to an end." On July 1st, under Sir Herbert Samuel as High Commissioner, there was installed the present Civil " Government." Political Zionism had made another stride forward.

But had it? There is a great question, a primary question, being asked in Palestine to-day, and that is " By what authority? " From what source does the Civil Government draw its power, its right to utter ordinances or proclamations, to legislate, to hold courts, to issue loans? By what right does it levy taxes, by what right summon an advisory council? There may be an answer to this in England, but in Palestine I found none.

Is it a Mandatory Government? The public has been given to understand that it *is* a Mandatory Government, executing the Mandate of the League of Nations, and drawing its authority from that body. In Mr. Churchill's wretched White Book of last June the air is thick with smug and hypocritical references to that Mandate, to the responsibilities and obligations it lays upon the Mandatory. Outward support has been given to this belief by the approval of the Mandate by the Council of the League of Nations, given at a sitting in St. James's Palace on July 24th, 1922.

But that approval was subject to the ratification of certain clauses dealing with the custody of the Holy Places of Christendom, and these clauses have not yet been ratified. Furthermore, the Mandate cannot come into force till such time as it has been approved and ratified by the General Assembly or Parliament of the League, sitting in a plenary meeting.

It follows therefore that if the present Government of Palestine is attempting to govern as a Mandatory Government—and certainly this impression has been conveyed to every soul in Palestine—by virtue of a Mandate which it has not yet received, and if justice is done may never receive, it is no Government, has no legal power behind its acts, and all its civil sentences, proclamations, borrowings, and what not are without any status.

A ceremony was held in Jerusalem, a few months after the " ratification " of St. James's, which is and has been since currently, and from a certain point of view usefully, described as the " Mandate " ceremony. Lord Allenby was present. But in point of fact, this ceremony was but the installation of Sir Herbert Samuel as High Commissioner. Sir Herbert Samuel himself has, I hasten to add, never given the ceremony any but its proper value. But the adepts of political Zionism have in their persuasive way bruited the ceremony about as the " Mandate " ceremony, the official opening of that felicitous era.

But again I ask : Is there a Mandate? The question is of such enormous importance from (to take but one point) the financial aspect that I am fortunate in being able to quote the decision on this matter of no less than a European Government, one, moreover, which is entirely neutral, and that is the Spanish Government.

In a despatch from the Foreign Minister in Madrid on a date in October, it is laid down (I quote the original Spanish) :

> Hasta ahora no ha variado la situacion pues el Manda to sobre Palestina entrera in vigor cuando todas las Potencias estén de acuerdo acerca de todos los puntos que abarca su texto, *y esto no ha sucedido todavia.*

That is to **say** :

> Up to the present the situation has not changed, since the Mandate over Palestine will come into force when all the Powers are in agreement upon all the points contained in its text, *and this has no yet occurred.*

This is clear enough for anybody. Even the Companions of Honour would have some ado in twisting this text for a White Book.

What follows from this situation? The present " Government " of Palestine, being without a Mandate, has, for example, no power to float a loan as a Mandatory. You know that it has expended about half of a loan it has not yet floated. In point of fact, its indebtedness upon advances is about £1,400,000. The proposed loan is one of £2,500,000. The major part of the advances have been made by the Crown Agents upon British security. So far as the drama has been revealed to you yet, the position was that the repayment of this sum depended upon the success of an unfloated loan.

But I believe you will agree that the situation is even more interesting, since the repayment of this sum depends upon a loan which the Palestine " Government " *cannot* float.   Should the Assembly of the League of Nations not approve the Mandate, the Palestine " Government " to all seeming will never be able to float it at all.   The £1,400,000 may go down as the largest individual subscription to the establishment of the " National Home."   Donor, John Bull, Esq., per Messrs. Lloyd George and Winston Churchill (Treaty Experts, Words Broken at the Shortest Notice.   References : The King of the Hedjaz, Sir Henry McMahon and others).

There is a second alternative.   Has the present " Government " been ruling as a Military Administration?   Sir Herbert Samuel was appointed High Commissioner and Commander-in-Chief over Palestine under an Order in Council.   Was it intended by making him Commander-in-Chief to give him military rank so that he might really hold his position as the Chief Officer in charge of Occupied Enemy Territory, or was the title a piece of customary formality?   An answer should again be quickly given.   But when Sir Louis Bols left Palestine the military régime was publicly treated as at an end.

The initials O.E.T.A. (Occupied Enemy Territory Administration) were removed from documents, from postage stamps, and everything of the sort.   Ordinances are enacted " by the High Commissioner for Palestine after consultation with the Advisory Council."   The whole attitude of the Government has been that it was on a different footing from the Military Administration.

Yet even if the present Government were a Military Administration, it seems clear that as such it could not float the proposed loan.   The Administrator of Occupied Territory cannot pledge the credit of that country in such a fashion.

If the Palestine Government is neither Mandatory (as it certainly is not) nor Military (as it does not seem to be), then what is it? Is it a Government?   Are any of its acts legal?   Is it being carried on by virtue of some Order in Council?   Does that empower the raising of taxes and creation of courts and all the rest?   The position should be made clear at once.

In Jerusalem on a November afternoon I put what seems to me one of the root questions in the Palestine affair to one of the prominent Jews of the Holy City. He is a man who is, I believe, on the point of abandoning political Zionism, of which he once was one of the chief advocates, for the dawning policy of self-reliant immigration.

He was completely frank in reply to my question, and I must say that amid some of the Jews in Jerusalem—and I include members and some of the staff of the Zionist Executive whom I met—I found a frankness which puts to shame our own Colonial Office.

"What on earth did you want the Balfour Declaration for at all?" I asked him.

"Well," he replied, "the truth is just this. The Jewish race is very idealistic, but it requires guarantees." This is, I think, a monumental phrase, and when he used it my friend had a lapse into political Zionism.

He went on: "The Jewish race is energetic, but also very pessimistic, and without the Declaration it might have thought Zionism a mere dream. We needed something palpable to win over the people and to gain their money. Suppose I had had to make a speech to an audience on behalf of the 'National Home.' I could have turned to them and said, 'There is something tangible in this. There is Britain's promise.' It was the power of a statement of that sort which enabled us to reach the people's hearts and the people's pockets."

Put that beside Mr. Winston Churchill's pretence of the reason for " formal recognition " of the National Home, and ask yourselves which rings true. There is nothing more scandalous in recent history than this giving of " Britain's promise " by her Ministers to be used as a bait for obtaining the money of unfortunate Jews. Whatever we do now, keep Britain's real promise to the Arabs or not, there are hundreds of thousands who will never hear the full facts and will believe that we have broken the only pledge of which they know.

I have called the Jews unfortunate. A large number of them certainly are. Think of what they have spent in Palestine. The latest round figures given by political Zionist leaders are £8,000,000. Think of that: £8,000,000 gone on a false start;

£8,000,000 taken out of their pockets on the basis of " Balfour " Declarations and false-bottomed White Books.

In Jerusalem I had access to some papers and they are very instructive. A Jewish Reorganisation Commission in a private report to Dr. Weizmann (and this was in 1921 when the £8,000,000 had not yet been reached) said : " The vast amounts expended have contributed in slight degree towards the establishment of a self-supporting Jewish community. . . . It was with deep regret we were obliged to conclude that the farms of the Jewish National Fund of which all Zionists have been taught to speak with pride were, from the standpoint of future national colonisation, of little value."

Who provided these great sums? The submerged Jew, the rank-and-file Jew everywhere, especially the Jew fighting with adversity in Poland, or Galicia, or Roumania, the Jews who give enormous quantities of lei or marks or levas, which mean slices out of their fortune to them and turned into pounds or dollars shrink to moderate contributions and must continually be renewed. So that now, having been exhausted, they can give little more, and unless further funds can be wrung from the Jews of the United States—Mr. Weizmann is on his way there— the whole movement will collapse.

The political Zionist movement is presented to the British public as a generous, impetuous, and uniform impulse of the Jewish race. It is nothing of the sort. Listen to the words of a Jew : " If the 16,000,000 Jews in the world were to equal the 300,000 Jews of Rumania—most of them very poor—they would produce at least £320,000. Nor would anyone be hurt by this effort, *for at present the average contribution per head for the redemption of the homeland is almost everywhere far below the cost of a tram-ride !* "

There are two main sources of subscription to the " National Home." One is the Jewish National Fund, the other is the " Keren Hayesod." The former of these exists for the specialised purpose of buying land. The latter is a Foundation Fund, into which all Jewish contributions the world over are to be canalised. In Palestine it is called the Keren Hageulah or Redemption Fund.

In Palestine itself, where restiveness and discontent with leaders is showing, Messrs. Yellin and Mehuhaz's National Council of

Jews was unable to get either money or accounts from the local committee of the Keren Hageulah for the last balance sheet, nor could they supply even a review of its work; the reason being that people would not pay and had no confidence in their leaders, and preferred to use such money as they had for social welfare organisations.

In their local currency the Jews of Lithuania in 1921 (which was the year in which the support of the printing-press currency countries seems to have reached its climax) increased their contributions more than eight times over. In Latvia they *wrung out* 1,800 *per cent. increase from their poor pockets ;* in Bessarabia 97 per cent.; in Rumania 242 per cent.; while in the United States the contributions fell 13 per cent.; in Great Britain 57 per cent., to £8,401.

The figures offered by the Keren Hayesod are more recent. In two years—that is to say, from the start of the fund till September 30th last—it had collected £614,692. The inexhaustible United States were last year asked to save the position, and out of that total about £400,000 came from them. Poland gave £22,000 and Britain £15,000; What a comparison these last two !

Taking the Jewish population of Britain as 310,000 (Jewish figures), their contribution a head a year works out at about sixpence. In Italy by the last report 700,000 lire had been promised (11d. nominal, about 3d. actual a head). In France 164,700 francs promised, about a franc and a half a head. French contributions to the Jewish National Fund in 1921 had worked out at three-fifths of a penny a head !

So two things stand out after making superabundant allowance for universal shortness of money. First, how far the Jews of the *world* are eager for political Zionism; secondly, the just value set upon the Declaration of all the Balfours by the Jews of Britain.

THE SLAV JEWS IN POWER.
THE COMMUNIST ELEMENT.

Just to sum up the financial balance a little. *British* expenditure for 1922-23 in Palestine and Transjordania, £400,000. Not for regular forces which would have to be paid wherever they were, but special Palestine expenses. Money advanced—British money—by Crown Agents on a *loan which cannot be floated,* say £1,000,000 now (it was £800,000 as far back as the end of March, and £1,000,000 is a small estimate). Therefore, say £1,400,000 for safety's sake between the two items. Good.

On the other side, from the political Zionists of the world contributions for the redemption of the homeland almost everywhere far below the cost of a tramway-car ride. Sacrifices by poor and humble Jews in Eastern Europe and the United States very great. Sacrifices, subscriptions from Sir Alfred Mond, Lord Rothschild, and other promoters of " Zionism for the British " in *strict proportion* to their fortunes? Still awaited. Jewish teachers in Palestine unpaid; Jewish medical work abandoned; Jewish education going on to the rates.

The close of a perfect year.

And just a glimpse again of what is occurring politically at this moment. British and politico-Zionists in angry and annoyed conclave. " What are we to do about all this? The Declaration, Winston's wretched White-Book, the Loan, the Mandate, all exposed ! "

" Never mind. Kisch (Colonel Kisch, you know, who has gone out as Political Secretary to the Zionist Executive in Jerusalem) is trying to get the Emir Abdulla of Transjordania contented with half the McMahon promises."

" I know, but then the Emir has absolutely no pull with the mass of the Arabs; they'll turn on him."

" What does that matter? It'll take a little time; the public won't tumble to the position. For heaven's sake, let us carry on at all costs and not go examining into things. We're telling the public now that the real object of the ' Home ' is to protect Egypt, British communications in the Near East, and so on.''

" Yes I know, but we're supposed to be acting or to be about to act in Palestine under a Mandate from the League of Nations, and using a Mandate to protect our own interests. When we do get it, won't that be a bit . . . you know what I mean?''

" Didn't I tell you not to examine into things?''

But let us examine into things. Let us take it at this low standard, assume that the National Home is to be run as a British Colony under the rose. Walk up the Jaffa Road in Jerusalem. At the top of the incline, opposite the gardens, affixed beside a doorway are two modest copper plates, never polished. Inside is a stairway leading to a floor of office rooms, tenanted by the Zionist Executive. Whom will you find there? You will find M. Ussischkin, M. Lurie, Mr. van Friesland, Mr. Jacobs and others.

The last two are in a class by themselves. Mr. van Friesland, a Zionist from Holland, conducts most of the negotiations between the Government and the Executive. He speaks excellent English. One could ask for no better, no more upright intermediary. He believes in a bridge being formed between East and West by the Jews, and says that the Zionists are so surrounded by teeming Arab populations that they must respect them. Mr. Jacobs is a young British Jew who fought with the Australians in the war, a very genuine, straightforward man.

But you would have a long way to search to get many more British Jews. You would find the corridors encumbered with immigrants who spoke plenty of languages, but not English, who come from strange sections of Eastern Europe and stare when they first see the Union Jack. To M. Ussischkin you would have to speak through an interpreter.

True, if there were Syrians there, you might have to do the same thing, but the Syrians would not have been presented to you as other than what they were. M. Lurie (a kindly man, I believe) would be obliged to confess to you, " Our school course lasts eight years. In the fifth year only do our children undertake the study of English. Hebrew is the basic language of instruction.''

Out of 4,242 Jewish school children in Jerusalem only 10 went there speaking English alone (9 spoke French). In Jaffa out of 822 there were 18 speakers of English alone.

From October 1st, 1921, to June 1st, 1922, out of 7,015 immigrants—adults this time—6,220 came from Eastern lands, mainly from Russian countries. From England there came 63. The British percentage is accordingly about .8 per cent.—eight British immigrants in 1,000.

In the main, therefore, what we are establishing at the cost you have seen in Palestine is not, as some of the silly folk from Manchester and elsewhere who are backing political Zionism believe, a British body but a Judæo-Slav one; not a London but an Odessa.

I am fully aware that in the hands of men like Mr. van Friesland, British interests would be absolutely maintained and his sense of gratitude to England for her help would make him our firm friend. But the point that I now must insist upon is that the power of men like Mr. van Friesland in the Zionist Executive is limited and that the power of the Executive itself and of such other benign persons as there may be in it is passing away.

The power to-day in Palestine, as far as Jewish power is concerned, is passing into the hands of the " Poale Zion," a body of young immigrants, and into the hands of the Council of Palestine Jews, which will by degrees be dominated by these same youths.

Mr. van Friesland and Mr. Jacobs (whose post is subordinate) are typical Girondins, men of moderation born to be superseded, till such time as men learn to instal what is the world's greatest necessity, passionate and turbulent moderation.

The new groupings in Palestine are Judæo-Slav; their processes are Judæo-Slav; their attitude upon life is Judæo-Slav; their mental intoxication is Judæo-Slav; and, should the present régime continue, when the first few years in contact with Britannic " emancipation " have been passed, all points to the constitution of a State not protective but perilous to Egypt, to the Near East, and to British communications.

It is of great importance to grasp the political tendencies of the Jewish youth, for they have the growing power, and consequently it is to them we must look for that devotion to British interests and the protection of Egypt and all the rest with which our pro-Zionists endow their future Jewish Commonwealth.

Their leader, probably the most important Jew in Palestine to-day, is M. Ben-Zwe. Now I had a long talk with M. Ben-Zwe, who is a very able man. M. Ben-Zwe had nothing to say about guarding British interests and so on, nothing at all. He had nothing to say against guarding them either. I don't think they come into his horizon. So long as they happened to march with Zionist interests I daresay he would do his best for them. I don't blame him or criticise him in the least.

He was quite frank that his ambitions were Hebraic, and crystallised the hope of himself and his companions thus : " Our desire is to bring all the workmen of Palestine into one body, into our ' Union,' the ' Ahadoth Ahavodah,' and to form one big union, to affiliate with the Vienna Group and ultimately with the Second International. That is our desire and we are very close to it. The goal at which we aim is a democratic co-operative State based on constructive Socialism.

" What we need is more and more immigration," he added. " When there are 300,000 Jews in Palestine then they will have the deciding voice in the fate of Zionism. And we trust that the influence of the members of our workers' organisations will grow more and more." This is a man who knows what he wants. He means that no Zionist Agency or Executive or anything of the sort in the bosom of Whitehall is going to tell them what to do, once they have encygh population in Palestine. And in Palestine their organisations will set the tune and fix the policy.

From M. Ben-Zwe I pass to M. Chaim Katz. Very different persons. Of course M. Ben-Zwe and his followers are not and cannot be that combination of advance-agents and buffers for the British Empire which our British Zionist-advocates of the Bootle school of politics believe them to be.

But in Palestine M. Ben-Zwe, on the other hand, has been unjustly called an extremist and other names of the sort. He knows more about the " Haganah," the Zionist Self-Defence force, than the authorities in Palestine like, but he wishes to get his organisations into the light of day and have them publicly recognised. Apart from this, he is a Constructive Socialist, who aims at a constructed Socialist State in Palestine, and he is, as he was careful to tell me, in close touch with Mr. Ramsay MacDonald and other members of the British Labour Party. You know now, at any rate, why Mr. Ramsay MacDonald makes no exhaustive references in his speeches to the text of the McMahon pledges to the Arabs. I am sorry to find that he too has received the freedom of the Vilayet of Churchill.

M. Chaim Katz is on a different platform from M. Ben-Zwe. He is an avowed Communist leader, who entered Palestine under an assumed name, and was recently arrested in Jaffa (I think it was) for re-entering the country clandestinely after expulsion. In fact, it was in the prison cell I saw him. He is a member of the Third International, the Russian organisation, and at the present moment there are probably 200 to 300 comrades of his in Palestine.

He tried, he said, to get his passport viséd by the British Consul in Vienna, but as this was refused he came in secretly.

" What else was I to do? " he said. " I am a student of agriculture, but I have worked as a mason " (he is a man of slight, rather pleasant appearance, not at all like a conventional mason), " and my intentions were, while working to gain my livelihood, to form a Workers' Protective Society, to get those of all races in this country to unite to defend their political interests.

" I am not out to create a Workers' State immediately. I do not suggest that men should go out into the street and start a revolution. The only way to achieve our aims is indeed by the dictatorship of the proletariat, but this cannot be attained through force. The right tactics for the moment are the professional movement, the forming of trade groups; it is a step towards the realisation of our ideas.

" Pay here is bad. A workman gets only 25 piastres a day often enough (about 5s. 3d.), and how can he keep a family on that? The Arabs, with their low standard, get along. We must teach them, and have their rate of pay raised too.

" I know that several leaders of the Jewish organisations do not share my opinions and are against my projects. I have nothing in common with M. Ben-Zwe. Many of the Jews here are Nationalists. But I think they are on the wrong road. It is no good tinkering with pseudo-Communism. You can't achieve Communist oases in a Capitalist desert."

I asked M. Katz why he felt the need of coming to Palestine to propagate his doctrines, as he had no relatives or ties in the country. His answer was interesting:

" It is better here than in the United States, for example, because here the workmen are grouped closely together, and there is a body upon which you can act. In the U.S. they are dispersed. Besides with the immigrants here I have natural connections of speech and ideas." " I don't see why I should be kept in prison," he added, " I've served my sentence. If I'm to be deported let me be deported, but at least let me be set free."

ENTER M. RUTENBERG.
THE BLEAK FACTS TO-DAY.

Of all the shameless things done by the Colonial Office in order to instal Zionism in Palestine at any cost either in money or in honour, none equals the signing in September, 1921, by the Crown Agents of the Rutenberg concessions. By these there was granted to M. Pinhas Rutenberg, Zionist Russian Jew, the right to harness the waters of the Jordan and the Oudja Rivers (the Oudja is in the Jaffa district) and the monopoly of the electric current thence drawn.

The lighting, the prospective transit and industrial power of Palestine were thereby handed over to the political Zionists, giving them, as the hapless Arabs say, a stranglehold over the country for seventy years.

These concessions were never thrown open to public tender, never examined on the spot by independent experts, never referred to the people of Palestine for approval or disapproval in any fashion.   The whole thing was carried through by the political Zionists on the one side and on the other by the Palestine Government, by Mr. Winston Churchill, and Sir John Shuckburgh and other permanent officials of the Colonial Office. Sir John Shuckburgh is one of those permanent officials badly in need of a little sound publicity. He is described in the Colonial Office list as " Accounting Officer for the Vote for Middle East Services."   Plenty to account for, indeed. But he has not accounted, does not, nor ever will account for the breaking of the McMahon pledges and of the solemn Allied Declaration of 1918.

Well, these treaty-experts put the thing through. The glories of the Rutenberg scheme were flashed in the eyes of the credulous Jews of the world. Pictures were painted them, especially in the United States, of Palestine rich with electrical energy and industry, of great Zionist engineers buckling to and bringing prosperity to lands to which neither Arab nor Gentile had given a thought. As was hoped, they subscribed sums of money to be repaid them in shares of the Rutenberg company when it should be floated. Naturally the Keren Hayesod advanced M. Rutenberg £7,500 out of the money given by the poor Jews of Eastern Europe. Naturally, too, none of the rich backers of Zionism rushed in with money.

Anyhow, we are now in 1923. Seventeen months have passed. The Jordan still flows undammed; the only thing which has been dammed is the small American and Eastern Jews' money, from the drip of which power will be drawn when the Rutenberg company is floated. But after seventeen months that company is still not floated, though it is daily promised for to-morrow.

The surface of the Oudja River is also undimmed by the rude industry of Rutenberg. All that exists so far in fact of the great enterprise I was able to focus within the finder of an ordinary Kodak last mid-November, on the outskirts of Tel-Aviv. Here, on the edge of the White-City-like township raised by Zionist endeavour (within whose streets and houses live 15,000 of the Zionists supposed to be "on the land "—often with six families to a house), forty or so young Zionist workmen are building a power-shed about the size of a mid-sized Chislehurst villa.

Lying in the open close by are two 500-h.p. German Diesel engines. Shed and engines comprise the totality of the Rutenberg scheme. Possibly the shed is built by now and the engines placed therein. I understand an underground electric cable has been laid to the homes which are a stone's throw away.

This, of course, unless the usual propaganda methods are altered, will be presently trumpeted the world over as an engineering achievement of incomparable grit and capacity. Later, light will be offered to Jaffa, of which Tel-Aviv is a suburb. It is an even chance that the municipality will refuse it, being a native municipality. Anyhow, this is all that has been done in seventeen months.

The promise of the future is about on a level with the results of the past. The Jordan is to be harnessed at enormous expense, and great cables are to bear electric power from below sea-level over pathless and lofty hills, *if* all goes well. But to what purpose? To light a few houses in four small towns where most of the population goes to bed with the dark, where the moon is the chief illuminant. Rutenbergians talk of 24,000-h.p., as a first instalment, too, to be garnered from the Jordan. This to supply some public electric light and water at 2¼d., and daily three to four hours' private light to a small body of Europeanised families at 7½d. per kilowatt-hour.

The Rutenberg undertaking, granting it were sound as a piece of engineering, which is a handsome grant, is financially preposterous unless there are to be large industrial demands for the current. I am letting you into a secret which many Zionists do not know when I tell you that the origin of it lay in the belief of some politico-Zionists, who knew nothing about the technical side of industry, that there would be huge demands, since their hope was to create in Palestine a great industrial centre which would seize the markets of the Near East and beyond, incidentally ousting Britain and other purveyors and making theirs a world-State.

However, that prospect has failed to unfold, and without industrial demands Rutenberg spells disaster. Zionists declare that their Palestine industries will come to its help, but, as for that, I inquired how many dividends of any sort had been returned by companies in Palestine last year. Could you guess? Two; just two. The Palestine Land Development Company and the Anglo-Palestine Company. The one returned 5 per cent.; the second 8 per cent., its actual profit being £25,000. Even if the two devoted companies were to light by electricity all the mortgages in Palestine, it is no outlook for M. Rutenberg.

The other companies in Palestine are mainly engaged in drawing heavily on their insufficient capital. The Zionist Budget itself (according to a secret report) is " drawn up on hope." The Colonies are mortgaged to at least 25 per cent. of their value, " and for five years a deficit of 20 per cent. will, it is reckoned, be incurred " on their running.

It is to this system and to these prospects that the people of Palestine *against their will* are tied by our Churchills and Shuckburghs. But there is worse to come. With Palestine there is always worse to come.

Some few months before the war in open competition, during January of 1914, a Greek financier named Mavromatis had obtained from the Jerusalem municipality formal concessions for electric lighting, tramways, electric energy, and water supply for the Holy City. He also had an option for similar work at Jaffa, and a draft agreement with the Turkish Government for the irrigation of the Jordan Valley on the principles adopted for the Nile. He had deposited in all £T12,000 and 180,000 francs in Paris and Palestine banks as security, all at full value, of course.

Since 1910 he had obtained and financed the tramways and electric light contract for Brussa, launched a 25,000,000 francs loan for the city of Constantinople in 1913 in conjunction with a French bank, a loan of 100,000,000 francs under the same conditions for the Ottoman Empire. Clearly a man of mark.

What happened when M. Mavromatis, before the Rutenberg concession was granted, approached the Palestine Government and later the Colonial Office, and asked either to be compensated or to be allowed to carry out his contracts *immediately*, further offering to deposit any more funds demanded, securing later the interest in his irrigation scheme of one of England's greatest engineers, who wrote letters on his behalf, securing also and promising British financial backing?

You would have, did you not know your Colonial Office, expected for Palestine's sake some sympathy, some interest in a scheme which was immediate and had money behind it, the reverse of Rutenberg's. But he was treated in the Churchill way. They told him first he had no right at all. Then they told him he had no right to proceed with his concession. Lastly, they told him he had *some* rights, but it was only an option and they wouldn't take it up. They told him he ought to come to an arrangement after meeting Rutenberg; that was their view. And then later on they said no purpose would be served by a meeting; that was their view.

In one letter Sir John Shuckburgh based a refusal on the Sèvres Treaty, and in another said the legal position was wholly undetermined till the Peace Treaty was operative. The Right Honourable Secretary said the water concession was divested of any value or significance because Jerusalem, owing to Army work during the war, now had an effective water supply. (Effective! When I think of the water painfully dragged from wells in the chief Jerusalem hotel and of its empty taps.) Mr. E. F. L. Wood, Under-Secretary, while Sir John Shuckburgh was on holiday, recognised the concessionaire had rights. The Right Honourable Inventor of the Vilayet of Churchill, informed of this, could not go back on it, but said, " We recognise certain rights and will respect them *in so far as they exist."*   Just like his vilayet.

And so the matter drags on to this day, and the field is kept clear for M. Rutenberg, whose company is not floated, whose little power-house is supplying soon perhaps a little electric light to a little villa or two in a little township where a lot of devoted Zionists are a little off the land.

Printed by ALABASTER, PASSMORE & SONS, LTD., 83, Cannon Street, E.C.4. and published by Associated Newspapers, Ltd., London, E.C.4.